Character Education

Grade 5

By
Maria Backus, Rachel Couch, Ann Fisher,
Delana Heidrich, Lesa L. Rohrer

Illustrations by
Corbin Hillam

Cover Illustrations by
Corbin Hillam

Published by Frank Schaffer Publications
an imprint of

About This Book

Engaging students in thought-provoking activities that focus on good character behavior helps them develop a sense of purpose and guides them in making the right choices in life. The activities in this book will help develop Citizenship, Honesty, Fairness, Responsibility, Cooperation, Respect, Tolerance, and Perseverance. Each unit focuses on a single character trait. The qualities that define that trait are developed through short plays, take-home assignments, role-playing simulations, journal writing, and self-reflection activities. In addition, each unit includes the profile of a famous person whose life has served as a model of that particular character trait through his or her own actions and deeds. Activities that support the IRA, NCTE, and NCSS Standards have been identified in a Standards Correlation Chart at the beginning of each unit.

Use these activities to extend and enrich your existing character education program or to start a new one.

Author: Maria Backus, Rachel Couch, Ann Fisher, Delana Heidrich, Lesa L. Rohrer
Editors: Jerry Aten, Stephanie Orbec

 **Children's Publishing**

Published by Frank Schaffer Publications
An imprint of McGraw-Hill Children's Publishing
Copyright © 2004 McGraw-Hill Children's Publishing

All Rights Reserved • Printed in the United States of America

Send all inquiries to:
McGraw-Hill Children's Publishing
3195 Wilson Drive NW
Grand Rapids, Michigan 49544

Character Education—grade 5
ISBN: 0-7682-2795-X

1 2 3 4 5 6 7 8 9 PHXBK 09 08 07 06 05 04
The McGraw-Hill Companies

Table of Contents

Table of Contents

Table of Contents

Table of Contents

To the Teacher

Help your fifth graders learn what it means to be good citizens with the activities in this unit. Lessons are included which define citizenship and help students recognize admirable citizenship behaviors in the world around them. A glimpse back into history reveals a model citizen as well. A variety of formats are included to engage all students. Many of the lessons are tied to IRA/NCTE and/or NCSS Standards and enable you to cover important skills while teaching good character development. Emphasis is placed on real-life situations to which your fifth graders can easily identify.

Dear Parents and Caregivers,

Our fifth grade class is about to begin a study of good citizenship. We hope students will be talking about this character-building unit at home.

We will be discussing ways in which students can demonstrate character-building with good citizenship behavior in their home, classroom, community, and country. For example, at home, children can be kind and helpful with chores. In the community, students can recycle and donate goods to charity. Many more ideas will be explored as well.

Please be ready to discuss this topic with your child, and be ready to reinforce good citizenship behavior in action when you see it. Talk with your child about behaviors that are part of good citizenship, and be ready to share your own views as well.

Building better citizens together,

_____

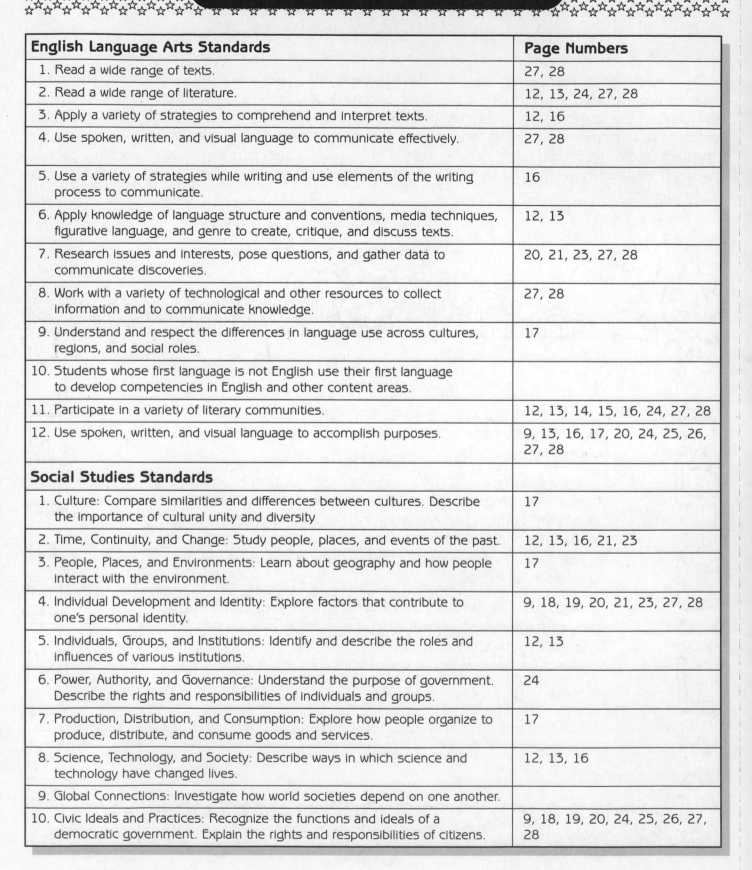

English Language Arts Standards	Page Numbers
1. Read a wide range of texts.	27, 28
2. Read a wide range of literature.	12, 13, 24, 27, 28
3. Apply a variety of strategies to comprehend and interpret texts.	12, 16
4. Use spoken, written, and visual language to communicate effectively.	27, 28
5. Use a variety of strategies while writing and use elements of the writing process to communicate.	16
6. Apply knowledge of language structure and conventions, media techniques, figurative language, and genre to create, critique, and discuss texts.	12, 13
7. Research issues and interests, pose questions, and gather data to communicate discoveries.	20, 21, 23, 27, 28
8. Work with a variety of technological and other resources to collect information and to communicate knowledge.	27, 28
9. Understand and respect the differences in language use across cultures, regions, and social roles.	17
10. Students whose first language is not English use their first language to develop competencies in English and other content areas.	
11. Participate in a variety of literary communities.	12, 13, 14, 15, 16, 24, 27, 28
12. Use spoken, written, and visual language to accomplish purposes.	9, 13, 16, 17, 20, 24, 25, 26, 27, 28

Social Studies Standards	
1. Culture: Compare similarities and differences between cultures. Describe the importance of cultural unity and diversity	17
2. Time, Continuity, and Change: Study people, places, and events of the past.	12, 13, 16, 21, 23
3. People, Places, and Environments: Learn about geography and how people interact with the environment.	17
4. Individual Development and Identity: Explore factors that contribute to one's personal identity.	9, 18, 19, 20, 21, 23, 27, 28
5. Individuals, Groups, and Institutions: Identify and describe the roles and influences of various institutions.	12, 13
6. Power, Authority, and Governance: Understand the purpose of government. Describe the rights and responsibilities of individuals and groups.	24
7. Production, Distribution, and Consumption: Explore how people organize to produce, distribute, and consume goods and services.	17
8. Science, Technology, and Society: Describe ways in which science and technology have changed lives.	12, 13, 16
9. Global Connections: Investigate how world societies depend on one another.	
10. Civic Ideals and Practices: Recognize the functions and ideals of a democratic government. Explain the rights and responsibilities of citizens.	9, 18, 19, 20, 24, 25, 26, 27, 28

Name _____

What Is Citizenship?

You probably already know that you are a citizen of your family, your classroom, your community, and your country. When you act in a way that identifies you with this group and are helpful to the group, you are showing good citizenship.

Here are some ways in which adults may display good citizenship in some of the groups to which they may belong:

- **Country**—Voting in national elections, running for office, paying taxes on time, serving in the armed forces.
- **Community**—Picking up trash in a city park, volunteering at a hospital, giving food or money to homeless shelters.
- **Workplace**—Giving someone a ride home from work, cooperating with other workers, completing jobs correctly and on time.
- **Family**—Doing someone's laundry, emptying the trash, saying kind words to another family member.

List examples of ways you show good citizenship on the blank lines below.

In your country:

1. _____

2. _____

In your community:

1. _____

2. _____

In your classroom:

1. _____

2. _____

In your family:

1. _____

2. _____

Name _____

Identify the response you think would be best in each situation below. Think about how to show good citizenship each time. Write the letter of the best answer next to each action. You will use some letters more than once. Be ready to discuss your answers with your classmates.

Action

_____ 1. You're walking down the street and notice a child crying because she's lost her balloon.

_____ 2. A friend accidentally sat in a wet seat on the bus, and now her jeans look funny.

_____ 3. Your little brother climbed up in a tree and is too scared to come down.

_____ 4. An elderly man just fell down in the grocery store.

_____ 5. You notice that there's fire coming from your neighbor's upstairs window.

_____ 6. A neighbor girl is riding her bike past your house. The chain comes off her bike and she is unable to ride it anymore.

_____ 7. Someone on the elevator has the hiccups and is very embarrassed about it.

_____ 8. You and your siblings are home alone. Your younger sister accidentally swallows some poisonous cleaning products.

Responses

A. Stop and ask if the person needs help.

B. Call 9-1-1

C. Don't do or say anything.

D. Tell your teacher or parents about the situation.

E. Try to find someone nearby to help.

Name _____

Good Citizen Hunt

Think about examples of good citizenship you have seen or learned about from real life, television, movies and books. Hunt down situations and file the four reports below.

Real-Life
Good Citizenship Report

On _____ I saw
date

_____ acting
person's name

as a good citizen. This person was

_____
action

_____.

Signed, _____
your name

Television
Good Citizenship Report

On _____ I saw
television show

_____ acting
character's name

as a good citizen. This person was

_____
action

_____

Signed, _____
your name

Cinema
Good Citizenship Report

In _____ I saw
movie title

_____ acting
character's name

as a good citizen. This person was

_____
action

_____.

Signed, _____
your name

Literary
Good Citizenship Report

In _____ I read about
book title

_____ acting
character's name

as a good citizen. This person was

_____
action

_____.

Signed, _____
your name

0-7682-2795-X *Character Education*

Profile of a Good Citizen

Anne Sullivan

A teacher of blind students, Anne Mansfield Sullivan was a great American citizen. She improved the lives of her pupils. While her name may not sound familiar, you have probably heard of her most famous student, Helen Keller. Anne had a difficult childhood. She was born into a very poor family and her brother was crippled from tuberculosis. Her father was very poor and was often mean-tempered and abusive. Her mother died when she was only eight years old. After that, Anne lived in a state orphanage.

School at first was very difficult for Anne. Her vision was weakened from a childhood illness. After she had several operations to help her regain her vision, she learned quickly at the Perkins Institute for the Blind. Soon she was given the job of helping other students. She learned to communicate with blind students.

After graduating from the Institute, Miss Sullivan moved to Alabama to become Helen Keller's personal teacher and companion. Helen Keller marked that day as "the most important day of my life." Helen was both blind and deaf and was just seven years old. Anne first had to teach Helen to be disciplined and to obey. Then she taught her the manual alphabet and the Braille alphabet. The first word Anne taught Helen was d-o-l-l. She placed a doll in one of Helen's hands, and spelled the word in the other. After a few weeks, Helen learned that everything had a name. During that summer Anne helped to unlock the mysteries of words and language for Helen. To Helen, it brought much joy.

With Anne's expert teaching skills and generous love, Helen soon learned many words and ideas. All who met them were amazed at Helen's ability to learn, and Anne's skillful teaching. Soon the two were traveling together, giving lectures, and raising money for the American Foundation for the Blind.

Toward the end of her life, Anne's eyesight failed again, but she continued to serve as Helen's companion. When Anne Sullivan died, she left behind a radically changed Helen Keller and a society more alert to the needs of blind people. Anne Sullivan was a citizen who made a difference!

Name _____

1. What made Anne M. Sullivan a great citizen?

   _____

   _____

   _____

2. It has been said that difficulties in life can either make you better or bitter. Which way did Anne's childhood affect her?

   _____

   _____

   _____

3. How long did Anne Sullivan stay with Helen Keller? What do you think made her so committed to her student?

   _____

   _____

   _____

4. What changes do you think may have occurred in the way blind students are taught from Anne Sullivan's time until now?

   _____

   _____

   _____

5. Name professions, in addition to teaching, in which people try to improve society.

   _____

   _____

   _____

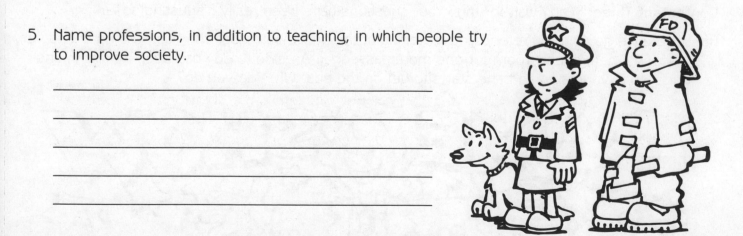

Game Show Sham

Setting: *A TV game show studio*

Characters: *Host, three contestants, studio audience*

Host: Welcome, contestants and audience to another edition of the sensational *Game Show Sham*. You may recall that last week's show was called *How To Be a Terrible Teacher*. Before that, we featured *How To Be a Terrible Student*. Well this week, folks, are you ready for this? Tonight's show is called *How To Be a Terrible Citizen*. Contestants are you ready? Audience are you ready?

(Both groups respond with cheers)

Host: Okay, Contestant Number One. Suppose you were in this situation: You and your brother are fighting over the last fresh juicy apple in the house. You, being a terrible citizen (of course), grab it away from your brother. You take a big bite into it and discover a small brown worm. As a terrible citizen, what do you do next?

Contestant One: Well, sir, I would not tell my brother about the worm. I'd tell him I changed my mind and want to share the rest of it with him. I'd tell him to close his eyes, open his mouth and take a big bite, and then . . .

Host, interrupting: That's quite enough, Number One. I think we'd all agree that you're a terrible citizen at home. Thank you for that excellent answer. Remember, audience, that you'll be voting at the end of our show on which player you think is the most terrible citizen. Let's turn now to Player Number Two. What would you do if your best friend asked you to lie to her mother about something she did at school?

Contestant Two: That's easy. Of course, I'd lie. First, I'd lie to her mother and then I'd lie to my friend, telling her that I *didn't* lie to her mother so that she'd really be confused and really get mad at me!

Host: Okay, Number Two. I'm not sure if I follow you, but lying is one great way to be a terrible citizen, so we must give you credit for that! Your turn, Number Three.

Contestant Three: I can't wait for this. Your questions have been really disgusting so far!

Host: Here we go, Three. Pretend you're waiting at the public bus stop. The bus pulls up and is very crowded. There is only room for one more passenger. An elderly lady has been waiting in line longer than you have, and she starts to get on the bus. What do you do?

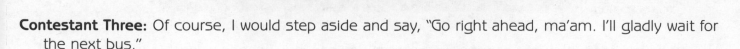
Contestant Three: Of course, I would step aside and say, "Go right ahead, ma'am. I'll gladly wait for the next bus."

Host, in disbelief: You would? But you're supposed to be a *terrible* citizen, not a *good* citizen when you play this game!

Contestant Three: Sorry. I just can't handle this sham of a game show anymore. Contestants One and Two, what do you say? Shall we go write a new game show of our own? It can't be any worse than this one!!!

Audience: Cheers and applause.

Contestant One: Hooray for you, Number Three. It was easy to answer those stupid questions, but I didn't enjoy it. I'm glad you are going to write a new program.

Contestant Two: So am I! We'll need lots of ideas on how to be a good citizen if we're to make a new show.

Contestant Three: So we will. Let's ask the studio audience for help. Audience, would each of you take a piece of paper and write down a situation in which a player needs to make a choice on what is the *right* thing to do? Write the situation in the form of a question where the contestant needs to describe what a good citizen should do. Then we'll let a new show begin!

Have everyone in the class follow the instructions given by Player Three at the end of the skit. Read the situations aloud and take turns answering them. How is this positive game more helpful and instructive than the original game?

_____

_____

_____

_____

0-7682-2795-X *Character Education*

Name _____

You have already thought about ways in which you can show good citizenship in the time and place in which you live. This assignment asks you to think about how people demonstrated good citizenship in the past.

Pretend you are a newspaper writer in your town in the 1890s. What was happening back then? If possible, use your library resources or the internet to find actual "current events" of that time period. Learn about what inventions were new, and which were non-existent. Think about how someone your age living in that year would display good citizenship. Then write a fictitious newspaper article that tells the public about someone who demonstrated excellent citizenship.

_____

_____

_____

_____

_____

_____

How would the action you described above fit in with today's assessment of what it takes to be a good citizen? Have times changed? Or does good citizenship today mean the same thing it meant during the 1890s?

_____

_____

_____

_____

_____

Name _____

Some of the ways in which you demonstrate good citizenship may be different from the ways in which students in another country demonstrate good citizenship. For instance, you might offer to help an elderly neighbor rake leaves. That would not be possible, however, for someone who lives in a desert.

Wait while the teacher divides all the students in your class into five groups and assigns one city below to each group. Learn about life in your location including the types of work people do, their methods of transportation, the foods they eat, etc. Then as a group, define three ways in which someone your age might display good citizenship that are different from ways you would demonstrate it where you live. Be ready to share what you learned and what you wrote with the rest of the class.

1. Reykjavik, Iceland
2. Santiago, Chile
3. Shanghai, China
4. Abuja, Nigeria
5. Sydney, Australia

Calling All CItizens!

Do you think you know how to be a good citizen? Are you ready to help others learn, too? Read each situation below. Volunteer to work with one or more classmates to act out one of the situations in front of your classmates. Show how you can encourage each other to become better citizens.

1. You are so excited! You just earned your first 100% on a science quiz! You can't wait to tell your best friend, Sammy. During your next class period, you and Sammy will both be in the library. You are on your way to the library and you see Sammy sitting at the front table. You are just about ready to blurt out your good news. Act out the parts of Sammy and yourself. Think about appropriate behavior for the library.

2. Nikki, Jason, and Tamara are walking home from school together. Nikki complains about all the things that their teacher does that she doesn't like. She gets the idea of writing a petition and asking students to sign it. The petition would ask the principal to make the teacher do a better job. Nikki asks Jason and Tamara for their opinions about the petition. What should Jason and Tamara say? Act out the parts of Nikki, Jason, and Tamara.

3. Tim is being a good citizen at home by helping his dad clean out the garage. They are sorting things out to keep, things to donate to others, and things to throw away. There is a big pile of newspapers, envelopes, and files, so Tim decides to burn these in their burn barrel. Shortly after Tim starts the fire, his neighbor, Mr. Stone, comes out. He reminds Tim and his father that he has breathing problems and that the smoke makes him ill. How should Tim and his dad reply to Mr. Stone? Act out the parts of Tim, his father, and Mr. Stone.

4. Herb, Sal, and Cindy walk to school together every day. They have to cross a street where there is no crossing guard. The traffic is supposed to stop at a stop sign, and when it does, the three friends can safely cross the street. But many mornings, there are cars that do not stop at the stop sign. Herb, Sal, and Cindy are getting frustrated about this problem. What can they do to try to improve this situation? Act out the parts of Herb, Sal, and Cindy as they brainstorm together.

5. On Monday, Jan invited Kendra to come home with her on the bus after school that Friday to spend the night. Kendra asked her mom for permission. Kendra's mom agreed, as long as she knew that Jan's parents would be home. On Tuesday, Kendra told Jan she could come as long are her parents would be home. Jan said they would be. It's Friday morning at school. Jan tells Kendra that her parents need to go out of town to visit her sick grandfather, but that it is still okay with her parents to have Kendra over. Kendra really wants to go to Jan's, but she knows her mother would not approve of the new plan. What should she do? Act out the parts of Jan, Kendra, and Kendra's mother.

6. Kevin lives on Maple Street in between Mark and Mrs. Lopez. Kevin and Mark want to start their own band. Kevin is learning to play drums, and Mark is taking guitar lessons. Mark is not allowed to practice his guitar after 9 P.M. because it might be too noisy for the neighbors. Kevin is allowed to practice his drums whenever he wants, but Mark knows that the sound bothers Mrs. Lopez. How should Mark handle this situation? Act out the parts of Kevin and Mark.

7. On Wednesday morning, John invites Travis to go to Friday night's football game with him. Travis accepts his invitation. On Thursday morning, Kay asks Travis to go to a concert with her on Friday night. Travis really wants to go to the concert, but he already made plans with John. What should he do? Act out the parts of John, Travis, and Kay.

8. Two people, Deb Riley and Trudy Mann, are running for the office of city mayor. You think that Deb would be a very good mayor, but you don't like some of the ideas Trudy has. Deb learns about you and asks you to help with her campaign. What might she ask you to do? How would you respond? Act out the parts of Deb Riley and yourself.

Dinnertime Duel

Here's a fun activity for you to make and take home to your family. Cut out each box, fold in half, and place in a jar. Sometime during your family time (such as at the dinner table, or before bedtime) pass the jar to someone in your family. Ask someone to take out one slip of paper without looking. That person then opens it and reads it to the rest of the family. Every family member should try to finish the sentence in a different way. Get ready for some family learning and fun with citizenship!

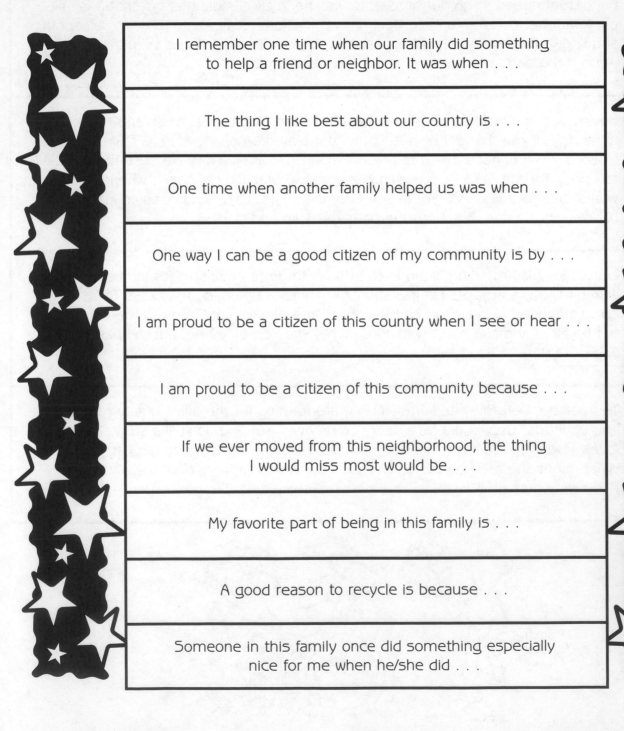

I remember one time when our family did something to help a friend or neighbor. It was when . . .

The thing I like best about our country is . . .

One time when another family helped us was when . . .

One way I can be a good citizen of my community is by . . .

I am proud to be a citizen of this country when I see or hear . . .

I am proud to be a citizen of this community because . . .

If we ever moved from this neighborhood, the thing I would miss most would be . . .

My favorite part of being in this family is . . .

A good reason to recycle is because . . .

Someone in this family once did something especially nice for me when he/she did . . .

In this game, students will conduct research, learn about history, and best of all, study some great citizens of the past! Here's how to play:

1. Select a list of famous citizens so that there is one name for each student. Two sample lists appear on the next pages.

2. Print out the list and cut the names apart, folds each name in half, and places the names in a paper bag or other container.

3. Instruct each student to draw one name from the bag and keep its identity a secret.

4. Then have each student find biographical information about their citizen. Each student only needs a few key facts. Ask each student to write down three important, distinctive facts about their citizen. These facts should be handed to the teacher.

5. Make one master list using information from student research. You may choose to use one, two, or all three of the facts. Copy the master list into a single document, mixing up the facts and leaving space between them for "signatures."

6. When you are ready to play the game, ask each student to wear an easy-to-read label that bears the name of the person that they have researched. Distribute a copy of your "master list" to each player. Upon your signal, each student circulates around the room trying to obtain "signatures" of people who are described on the master list. For example, suppose that Toby was assigned to research Benjamin Franklin. For his three facts, he wrote:

   1) This famous person lived much of his life in Philadelphia, PA.

   2) This person performed important experiments with electricity.

   3) He wrote *Poor Richard's Almanac*.

   Toby's teacher compiles two of these facts (#1 and #3) with two facts from every other student in the class. Ashton reads the master list and thinks that Toby's character, Benjamin Franklin is the author of Poor Richard's Almanac. So Ashton asks, "Toby, can you sign my page as the author of Poor Richard's Almanac?" Toby, of course, agrees and signs the name, Benjamin Franklin in the appropriate space on Ashton's master list. Students should not ask general questions such as, "Is there any fact on my list which you can autograph?"

7. The first player to collect signatures for every fact is the winner. Or, the winner is the student who collects the most signatures before time runs out.

Citizen Signatures

Use this list to play *Citizen Signatures*. This list contains the names of 30 famous American citizens. Included are governmental leaders, inventors, athletes, and more.

George Washington	Ronald Reagan	Sandra Day O'Connor
Thomas Edison	Henry Ford	Ulysses S. Grant
Abraham Lincoln	Harriet Beecher Stowe	George Washington Carver
Mary Lou Retton	Jim Thorpe	Susan B. Anthony
Eleanor Roosevelt	Daniel Boone	Andrew Carnegie
Jefferson Davis	John Paul Jones	Francis Scott Key
Dolley Madison	William Penn	Dwight Eisenhower
Molly Pitcher	Richard Byrd	Luther Burbank
Squanto	Woodrow Wilson	Neil Armstrong
Sally Ride	Thomas "Tip" O'Neill	John Wayne

Citizen Signatures

Use this list to play *Citizen Signatures*. This list contains the names of 30 famous citizens from around the world. Included are governmental leaders, inventors, athletes, and more.

Hammurabi	Pericles	Plato
Vasco de Balboa	Hans Christian Anderson	John James Audubon
Roger Bacon	Leonardo da Vinci	Christopher Columbus
Vasco da Gama	William Shakespeare	Isaac Newton
Johann S. Bach	Thomas Jefferson	Robert Fulton
Samuel Morse	Florence Nightingale	Louis Pasteur
Mahatma Gandhi	Franklin D. Roosevelt	Winston Churchill
Jonas Salk	Jane Austen	Agatha Christie
Margaret Thatcher	Samuel de Champlain	Harriet Tubman
Lucille Ball	Henry Hudson	John Calvin

0-7682-2795-X *Character Education*

Name _____

Once upon a time, in the Land of Good Citizenship, a new queen came to rule on the throne. After a short time in power, she called a meeting of all the people in her land.

"I am weary of all the good behavior of my subjects," the queen announced. "I am weary of all the kindnesses that you show to one another. I am weary of your devotion to the throne and this land." she continued. "I hereby proclaim that for one week, no one is allowed to behave like a good citizen," the queen declared.

And so, the loyal subjects obeyed. But you see, loyalty in itself was an act of citizenship and so was forbidden. For one week, the citizens tried very hard to not behave themselves. Food was stolen from the royal pantry. Servants didn't report to work. The royal throne did not get cleaned. The farm produce was not harvested, nor was it brought to the castle.

At the end of one week, the tired, hungry, tattered queen again appeared before her subjects (who were still very loyal, by the way).

"Good citizens," she began, "indeed I have made a grave error. While I earlier stated that I was tired of your good citizenship, I find today I am even more tired from trying to rule this kingdom on my own. You see, I've learned that . . ."

Finish the queen's statement Then add another complete thought to the dialogue.

_____

_____

_____

_____

_____

_____

Name _____

Reflecting Back

1. To me, being a good citizen means . . .

_____

_____

_____

_____

2. Concerning good citizenship in your home and your classroom, rate yourself on these behaviors:

   1 = I don't usually display this behavior.
   2 = I sometimes exhibit this behavior.
   3 = I almost always behave in this manner.

   _____ I follow the rules set by my parents and teachers.

   _____ I volunteer for jobs around the house and classroom.

   _____ I clean up after myself and put trash in the wastebasket.

   _____ I do my chores and homework on time.

   _____ I follow safety rules and procedures.

   _____ I work cooperatively with others.

   _____ I respect the authority of my parents and teachers.

3. Finish this sentence. I think I could improve my citizenship at home or school by...

_____

_____

_____

4. Here are some new ways in which I can show good citizenship:

   In my community I can . . . _____

   _____

   In my country I can . . . _____

   _____

Name _____

Keep a log for one week of good citizenship that you see in yourself and in others by completing this journal.

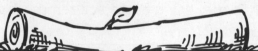

Day of week	Examples of good citizenship in myself	Examples of good citizenship in others
Sunday		
Monday		
Tuesday		
Wednesday		
Thursday		
Friday		
Saturday		

On the back of this page, create a new log showing how you plan to show good citizenship during the next week.

Students can practice good citizenship throughout the entire school year when you introduce them to these extension activities.

- Collect quotations and slogans that promote good citizenship. Occasionally. write one quotation on the chalkboard and discuss its meaning. Talk about how the words encourage people to become better citizens. Some sample quotations include:

  - The measure of a man's real character is what he would do if he knew he would never be found out.

    —*Lord Macaulay*

  - The great use of a life is to spend it for something that outlasts it.

    —*William James*

  - If I take care of my character, my reputation will take care of itself.

    —*Dwight L. Moody*

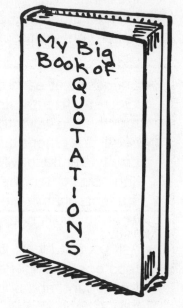

- Ask students to create family posters. Each student should write the names of family members and add words to describe them or explain their abilities and interests. Encourage students to celebrate the good times in their families. Magazine pictures or computer clip art can be used as illustrations. When posters are complete, send the posters home with students where the student can personally present his poster to his family.

- Recognize that a part of good citizenship is learning about the history, laws and leaders of the country. Pair your students, then assign one important national leader (past or present) to each pair. Give your students one to two weeks to learn about the event or person from textbooks, newspapers, family experts, the Internet, or other sources. At the end of this time period, ask each pair of students to make a poster illustrating and summarizing the major facts about that person. Have them present their posters to the class.

- Challenge your students to try to surprise their families at least once a week by doing some chore in the home without being asked. Allow them time to report the results to the class.

- Suggest that each of your students become a "Secret Citizen" in the classroom. Brainstorm together on ways that students can quietly do good deeds for other students or the teacher. Examples: Empty the trash without being asked. Sweep the floor. Straighten the classroom library. Remind students that these good deeds should be done only when they will not be disrupting other students.

- Ask your students to devise a plan for collecting box tops or coupons. Perhaps they can offer to collect, then count, and bundle them before turning them into school officials. They may want to design and print a brochure advertising their program. Talk with students about special projects that will be funded with the money they help to raise

- Talk about school situations/places in which good manners are needed in order to display good citizenship. Examples: waiting in line at the cafeteria, studying in the library, working at the teacher's desk, etc. Ask each student to choose a place or situation and draw a picture showing a person using good citizenship. Instruct students to include a caption under the picture that will help others to remember to practice good citizenship. Post the pictures on a classroom wall.

- Role-play dinner-table situations where good manners are important. Practice *please, thank you, please pass the carrots*, and so on. Encourage students to use these manners at home and in the school cafeteria..

Honesty

We chose our profession for a myriad of reasons. Because we are teachers, we are eager to pass on our own respect for books and knowledge and learning. We know the value of exercising brains as well as bodies. We accept the responsibility of maintaining an educated democratic citizenry and effective employee base. Perhaps most importantly, teachers strive to give the next generation the tools to become people of good character.

Education provides the basis for good decision-making. Stating a problem, evaluating choices, and making a plan for action all require critical thinking skills. As we teach these skills, we prepare the next generation to be honest people of good character.

This unit is designed to simplify the teaching of the character trait honesty. Within its pages, students are introduced to the definitive behaviors associated with being truthful and real. Through interactive reading, writing, and speaking activities tied to national language arts and social studies standards, students explore and practice such behaviors. You and your students are certain to enjoy and benefit from the journey.

Dear Parent or Guardian:

Our class is beginning a character-building unit on honesty. We will explore the behaviors associated with being truthful through interactive reading, writing, speaking, and role-playing activities. I invite you to continue the focus on honesty at home. Challenge your child to tell even difficult truths. Discuss the benefits of being trustworthy. Demonstrate honesty yourself. Invite your child to share with you the honesty-focused activities we conduct in the classroom.

Being honest will empower your child to make good decisions. Thank you for your assistance in reinforcing this valuable character trait at home.

Sincerely,

_____

English Language Arts Standards	Page Numbers
1. Read a wide range of texts.	50
2. Read a wide range of literature.	34, 35, 36, 37, 46, 50
3. Apply a variety of strategies to comprehend and interpret texts.	31, 32, 35, 36, 37, 40, 41, 46, 50
4. Use spoken, written, and visual language to communicate effectively.	31, 32, 33, 35, 36, 37, 38, 39, 40, 41, 43, 44, 45, 46, 48, 49, 50
5. Use a variety of strategies while writing and use elements of the writing process to communicate.	31, 32, 33, 34, 38, 39, 47, 48, 49, 50
6. Apply knowledge of language structure and conventions, media techniques, figurative language, and genre to create, critique, and discuss texts.	35, 38, 39, 47
7. Research issues and interests, pose questions, and gather data to communicate discoveries.	32, 33, 40, 41, 43, 44, 45, 47, 48, 49, 50
8. Work with a variety of technological and other resources to collect information and to communicate knowledge.	49, 50
9. Understand and respect the differences in language use across cultures, regions, and social roles.	40, 41, 49
10. Students whose first language is not English use their first language to develop competencies in English and other content areas.	
11. Participate in a variety of literary communities.	36, 37, 40, 41, 42, 49, 50
12. Use spoken, written, and visual language to accomplish purposes.	31, 32, 33, 35, 36, 37, 38, 39, 40, 41, 46, 47, 48, 49, 50

Social Studies Standards	
1. Culture: Compare similarities and differences between cultures. Describe the importance of cultural unity and diversity.	32, 34, 35, 36, 37, 49
2. Time, Continuity, and Change: Study people, places, and events of the past.	34, 35, 46, 50
3. People, Places, and Environments: Learn about geography and how people interact with the environment.	34, 35, 46, 50
4. Individual Development and Identity: Explore factors that contribute to one's personal identity.	31, 33, 38, 39, 42, 43, 44, 45, 47, 48
5. Individuals, Groups, and Institutions: Identify and describe the roles and influences of various institutions.	34, 35, 49, 50
6. Power, Authority, and Governance: Understand the purpose of government. Describe the rights and responsibilities of individuals and groups.	31, 32, 34, 35, 36, 37, 38, 39, 40, 41, 42, 47, 48, 49, 50
7. Production, Distribution, and Consumption: Explore how people organize to produce, distribute, and consume goods and services.	
8. Science, Technology, and Society: Describe ways in which science and technology have changed lives.	34, 35
9. Global Connections: Investigate how world societies depend on one another.	
10. Civic Ideals and Practices: Recognize the functions and ideals of a democratic government. Explain the rights and responsibilities of citizens.	31, 32, 34, 35, 36, 37, 38, 39, 40, 41, 42, 47, 48, 49, 50

Name _____

Being Truthful, Trustworthy, and Honorable

Honesty is being truthful, trustworthy, and sincere. Being honest at home and at school makes you a person of honor and integrity. Explore the meaning of honesty by reading the definitions of each of the italicized words below. Then create a sentence using the word in an original sentence of your own.

truthful

1. telling the truth

2. in the habit of being honest

3. stating accurate facts

   Your Sentence: _____

   _____

trustworthy

1. reliable

2. dependable

3. trusted to tell the truth

   Your Sentence: _____

   _____

honorable

1. being true to your word

2. having an exceptionally good reputation

3. highly respected

   Your Sentence: _____

   _____

person of integrity

1. having a strong sense of what is right and good

2. being true to a high code of values

3. insisting on doing what is right

   Your Sentence: _____

   _____

Name _____

Honest Words and Actions

In complete sentences tell how an honest person would behave in each situation described here.

Sally's class takes a test while Sally is home sick. She knows that she will have to make up the test. Terri visits Sally after school. Terri has memorized the first five answers to the test Sally missed. Terri offers to share the memorized answers with Sally.

Sally's response:

_____

_____

_____

Kevin agreed to mow his elderly neighbor's lawn after school on Friday. Now three of Kevin's friends have asked him to go to the movies after school on Friday.

Kevin's response:

_____

_____

_____

Liz is a new student at Platte Valley School. She has made no friends yet, but a group of girls has invited her to a slumber party. At the slumber party, the girls are going to paint each other's nails, braid each other's hair, and do each other's make-up. Liz is active and athletic. She has no desire to wear braids, make-up, or fingernail polish. Actually, Liz considers herself a bit of a "tomboy."

Liz's response:

_____

_____

_____

Name _____

Observing other people acting trustworthy and honorable helps us recognize what it means to be honest. Think about times you have witnessed honesty and integrity. Write about specific instances in which each of the people mentioned below has demonstrated honesty. Participate in a class discussion about you and your classmates' examples of honesty in action.

A time your mother or father proved trustworthy:

A time your grandmother, grandfather, or other relative showed integrity:

A time one of your friends was sincere:

Nelson Mandela

Sometimes the honest man is rewarded with fame and honor. Sometimes the honest man finds himself in jail. Honesty led Nelson Mandela to fame, honor, and jail. In each situation, Mandela maintained his stronghold on the truth.

Nelson Mandela was born in South Africa, the son of a chief. He received a good education and was expected to accept political office as an adult. However, the truths Mandela learned about the historical treatment of his people convinced Mandela to become a freedom fighter instead.

Although whites made up a minority of the population, they ruled South Africa. Laws were passed that made life unfair for Indian and black people living in South Africa. Mandela read about the many struggles his people had endured.

Mandela began to experience injustices similar to the ones about which he had read. The government began to pass laws in support of apartheid. Apartheid refers to policies meant to separate ethnic groups and keep power in the hands of whites. Under apartheid, blacks were not allowed to vote. They were not permitted to live in white neighborhoods or shop in whites-only stores.

Nelson Mandela knew that apartheid was wrong. He also knew that speaking the simple truth could endanger his life. He joined groups that opposed apartheid. He convinced people to join him in strikes, boycotts, and civil disobedience. He demanded voting rights, union rights, land ownership rights, and education rights for all people in South Africa.

Standing up for honor and truth was costly for Mandela. His law office was shut down. His travel was restricted. Finally, Mandela was imprisoned for 27 years. On at least two occasions during his time in prison, Mandela was offered a way out. If he would accept apartheid policies, he would be freed. Mandela refused. He would rather live a life of integrity in jail than one of deceit in freedom.

Thanks to the work Mandela and others did to expose the truth about apartheid, the world began to pressure South Africa to make a change. Gradually bans and restrictions were lifted. Black students could attend former all-white schools. It became legal to be a member of a political party that opposed apartheid. Finally, in 1990, Nelson Mandela was freed from prison.

In 1994, South Africa held its first *universal suffrage elections*. Citizens of all ethnicity were permitted to vote. People of all colors, cultures, and religions voted for the president of South Africa in 1994. And the winner of the election was Nelson Mandela! For five years, Mandela served as the democratically elected president of the country he believed in. Throughout his long struggle, he never lost sight of what was true and right. In the end, he proved the power of honesty can transform wrongs into rights.

Name _____

Questions to Consider and Discuss

Sometimes actions speak louder than words. Find examples from the story in which Mandela told the truth through his actions rather than his words.

_____

_____

_____

_____

_____

_____

_____

_____

_____

_____

Nelson Mandela spent 27 years in prison. He was taken away from his job, his family, and his cause. Still, he refused to leave prison if it meant he had to stop speaking the truth about the injustices in his country. Would you have made the same choice? Why or why not?

_____

_____

_____

_____

_____

_____

_____

_____

_____

_____

Reader's Theater

Old Man Brown Is Not Useless

Characters: *Carson, Daisuke, Sophie, Old Man Brown*

Scene One: the sidewalk outside of Old Man Brown's house

Sophie *(walking alongside Daisuke and Carson and pointing at Old Man Brown's house)*: That man's yard is an embarrassment to our entire neighborhood.

Daisuke: I know. Does he ever mow his lawn? Look at the weeds in his flower garden.

Carson: Come on guys, Old Man Brown's got to be at least 85 years old. How can you expect him to do yard work?

Sophie: I don't. Old men are useless. But if he cared at all about the appearance of this town, he'd hire some young guy to take care of his lawn.

Scene Two: Old Man Brown's house

Carson *(knocking on door until Old Man Brown appears)*: Hello, Old, umm, I mean, Mr. Brown. I'm one of your neighbors. I kind of wanted to talk to you about your yard.

Old Man Brown *(tears welling up in eyes)*: It's atrocious isn't it?

Carson: To be honest, sir, it is. Frankly, even the kids in the neighborhood are talking about what a mess it is.

Old Man Brown *(more tears and sadness)*: How long have you lived in this neighborhood, Son.

Carson: All my life. Ten years, I guess.

Old Man Brown: Then you never saw my place before I had my stroke. Those weeds over there choked out a prize-winning flower garden. Prize-winning, I tell you. Got my picture in some magazine. Them fruit trees in the corner along with a garden in the back fed half the neighborhood during troubled times, I just can't care for the yard anymore like I'd like to.

Carson: Some of the kids in town think it would be nice if you hired someone to do it for you. I'm no expert with flowers or fruit trees, but I can mow grass. And I could sure use a little spending money.

Old Man Brown: That's just it. I spent eighteen months in the convalescent hospital after my stroke. It cost me a pretty penny. I can't afford a groundskeeper. My grandson mows the lawn once a month or so, but he's a busy man. He's got an important job in New York City and all.

Scene Three: the baseball field

Daisuke: Hey, how come you missed practice yesterday?

Carson: I guess I wasn't feeling too well.

Sophie: It seems like you're never feeling too well. You've missed practice five times in the last month. If you keep missing practice, you're going to be as useless to this team as Old Man Brown is to his poor yard.

Daisuke: Actually, the old guy's yard has started looking pretty good. Have you been by there lately? He's even got the weeds out of the flowerbeds.

Sophie: Yea, well, he must have finally hired somebody to clean up that mess. I'm sure he isn't doing the work himself. The guy can barely walk. I'm telling you, Old Man Brown is useless.

Carson (screaming): OLD MAN BROWN IS NOT USELESS!

Sophie: What?

Daisuke: Yeah, what do you know about Old Man Brown?

Carson: To tell you the truth, I've been working on Old Man, I mean, Mr. Brown's yard. In exchange for the work I do, he's teaching me about flowers and fruit trees, grasses, and vegetables. He's a regular encyclopedia of knowledge about landscapes and gardening. I've got carrots coming up. And when we get the flowerbed done, we're going to enter it in a contest. I could get my picture in a magazine.

Sophie: Wow! It sounds like Mr. Brown does have some useful information. But what about baseball, Carson?

Carson: I know I've let you guys down. I guess its time for me to be honest with you and true to myself. I never liked baseball. I just like you guys. You're the only reason I even signed up for the team. I have the best time of my life working with Mr. Brown. Do you think it would end our friendship if I quit the team to spend more time grooming trees and mowing lawns and talking to a senior citizen?

Daisuke: Of course not, Carson.

Sophie: Just as long as you invite us to help you and Mr. Brown with that flowerbed so we can get our pictures in the magazine too.

(All three kids laugh)

Discussion Questions

1. Locate instances in which Carson was honest in the story.

2. When did Carson lie? When did he keep his friends from knowing the truth? Why might he have been less than honest with them?

3. Do you think Daisuke and Sophie have changed their views about elderly people by the end of the story? Did Carson's truthfulness help them do so?

Name _____

True Friends

Being honest helps us build positive relationships with other people. Think about the friends you play and work with. Look at the three prompts below. Choose one and write a paragraph response the prompt. Remember to use topic, supporting, and concluding sentences in your paragraphs.

Describe one of your most trustworthy friends. What makes that friend so trustworthy? What makes someone a "true friend?" How does a true friend differ from a friendly acquaintance? Tell about a situation in which you were a true, trustworthy, and honorable friend.

_____
_____
_____
_____
_____
_____
_____
_____
_____
_____
_____
_____
_____
_____

Name _____

Exaggerations, misleading information, and other forms of deceit can lead to confusion and chaos. Summarize a movie in which honesty saves the day in the end, clearing up confusion and chaos.

_____

_____

_____

_____

_____

_____

_____

_____

_____

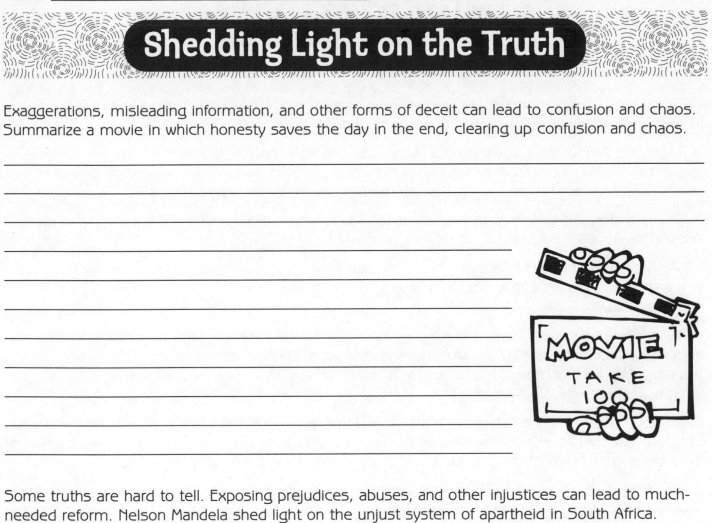

Some truths are hard to tell. Exposing prejudices, abuses, and other injustices can lead to much-needed reform. Nelson Mandela shed light on the unjust system of apartheid in South Africa. Write a short paragraph about a public figure who bravely exposed an injustice in historical or modern America.

_____

_____

_____

_____

_____

_____

_____

_____

_____

Honestly Acting

Choose pairs or groups of students to role-play the scenarios below. After acting out the portion of the scene described, students show what could happen next when one or more of the characters in the scene chooses to demonstrate honesty, integrity, and honor.

Karla and Anthony are discussing a class writing assignment. Karla tells Anthony it is just like an assignment from last year. Karla tells Anthony she is planning on turning in an exact copy of last year's writing rather than redoing the assignment this year. What happens next?

A small group of girls is gossiping about Tammy as she walks by. One of the girls in the group knows the stories are not true. What happens next?

A small group of boys is planning a trip to the movies on Saturday afternoon. One of the boys in the group knows his family does not have enough money to spend on the movies. What happens next?

Allison has two close friends, Martha and Daylella. Martha does not care for Daylella. In fact, she gets jealous and offended when Allison spends time with Daylella. In this scene, Allison and Daylella talk while Martha watches on the sidelines. When Daylella walks away, Martha confronts Allison. What happens next?

A group of boys and girls are playing soccer. Jorge overhears two boys laughing and making fun of Stanley's awkwardness on the field after a bad play. After the game, the two boys slap Stanley on the back and say sarcastically, "Good game. Thanks for winning it for us." What happens next?

Jennifer is shopping with her mother. While her mother looks at clothes, Jennifer wanders to the jewelry department. She sees a necklace she really wants. She doesn't have the money to buy the necklace, and her mother would not likely pay for such an unnecessary item. What happens next?

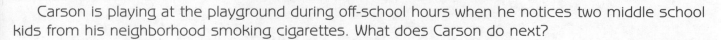

Carson is playing at the playground during off-school hours when he notices two middle school kids from his neighborhood smoking cigarettes. What does Carson do next?

Amanda is constantly worrying about her weight. She tells her friends she feels fat. Sally, one of her friends, notices Amanda often throws away the lunch her mother packs her everyday. Then after school, Amanda buys three or four candy bars from the candy machine before jumping on the bus. What will Sally do with her information?

Reginald and Emily are talking. Reginald notices Emily's breath is really offensive. What happens next?

Rick and David are brothers. Each morning, their parents leave for work before the boys leave for school. This morning, Rick and David are about to leave for school when Rick reminds David the table tennis championships are being held on television at 10:00. Rick suggests to David the boys "stay home sick" today to watch the championship games. What happens next?

Becky and Lindsay are working on a research paper together. The assignment requires six references so each girl is responsible to gather information from three sources. Lindsay only gathered information from two sources. She suggests to Becky they just add a book title to their reference page that they didn't actually use. What happens next?

A group of girls is begging Reta to join them at a sleep-over where all the girls are going to ride horses and make friendship bracelets. Reta is terrified of horses. What happens next?

Name _____

Honesty at Home

Having a "Heart to Heart"

Interview a member of your family to learn about his or her "true" self. Then share with your family member your own answers to the questions. Finally discuss interesting or surprising answers. Alternatively, use these questions to lead a whole-family discussion.

1. Tell me about a time you were tempted to make a bad choice, but chose to do the right thing in the end. What events, thoughts, or comments from others helped you make the right choice?

2. Have you ever stood up for a friend when others were making fun of that person? Tell me about it.

3. Tell me about a time your own honesty made you feel honorable and good.

4. Tell me about a person you admire for his or her integrity.

5. Have you ever supported a cause you believed in? What was the cause? In what ways did you support it? Why is the cause meaningful to you?

6. Tell me about your favorite childhood memory.

7. Tell me about a hobby or skill that you have enjoyed that few people know about.

8. Tell me about a childhood dream or desire.

9. What is the best part about being a part of our family?

10. Share with me one thing about you that I do not know.

Do-Track! Don't-Track!

After playing this game, you will be masters of the traits associated with honesty. Print off multiple copies of each game board (found on pages 44 and 45). Then follow the directions below.

Object of Game: Be the first player to make your way around both the Do-Track and the Don't-Track

Number of Players: Any number. Note: You will need one referee per player

Materials: One Do-Track and one Don't-Track per player
Seventeen coins or other markers per player

Rules:

1. Require each player to enlist the help of one referee.

2. Distribute a Do Track and a Don't Track to each player. Distribute seventeen coins or other markers.

3. At the word, "Go," each player begins to move down his or her Do-Track. To move down the track, the player must give an example that illustrates the trait described on that square.

4. When the referee is satisfied that an example accurately illustrates the trait listed on a square, the player places a marker on the square and moves on to the next square.

5. When a player has accurately illustrated each trait on the Do-Track, he or she moves on to the Don't-Track and proceeds in the same manner.

6. The first player to fill all squares on both the Do and the Don't Tracks with a marker wins the game.

Example:

Bill begins on Square One of the Do-Track: Do tell the truth.

Bill: I told the truth when I told my dad that I accidentally scratched his car door.

Referee: Acceptable example. Place your marker on the square and move on.

Bill is now on Square Two: Do Keep Your Promises

Bill: Keeping promises helps you keep friends.

Referee: That's true, but it is not an acceptable example of keeping a promise. Try again.

Bill: If you promise your mom you will do your homework before you play outside and you do just that, you have kept your promise.

Referee: Acceptable example. Move on.

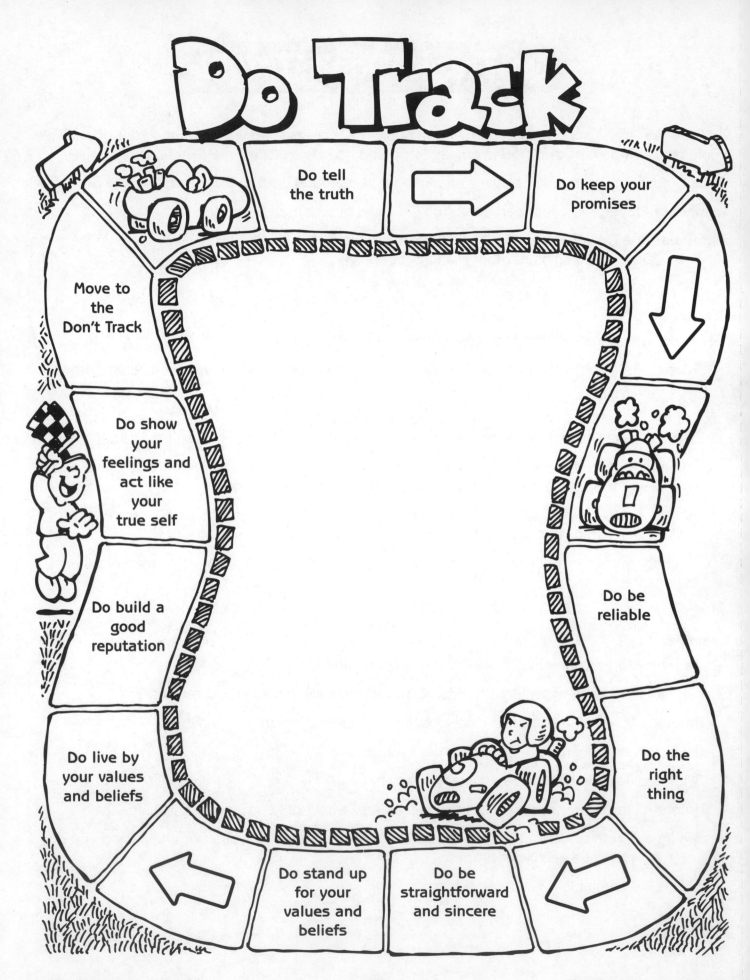

Do Track

Do tell the truth

Do keep your promises

Move to the Don't Track

Do show your feelings and act like your true self

Do be reliable

Do build a good reputation

Do the right thing

Do live by your values and beliefs

Do stand up for your values and beliefs

Do be straightforward and sincere

0-7682-2795-X *Character Education*

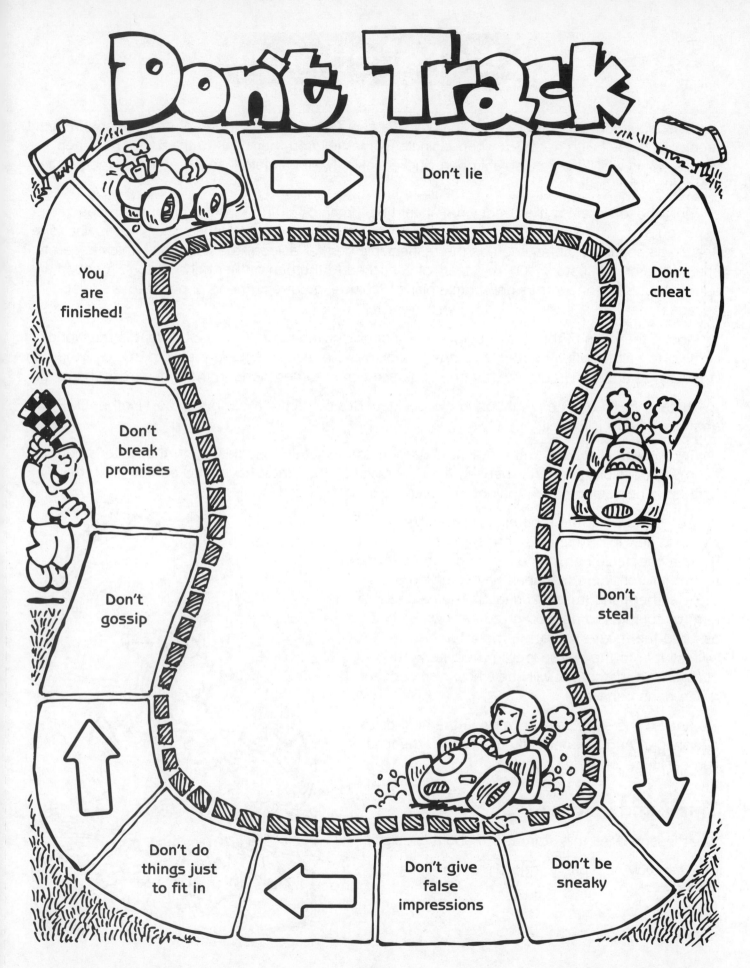

0-7682-2795-X *Character Education*

It's Perfectly True

It happened in a hen house, in the quiet of a cool October evening. A very respectable hen sat grooming herself with her beak when a single feather fell from her back to the floor of the hen house. "All is well," the respectable hen clucked jokingly, "If I should lose a feather, all the prettier I become, I suppose."

Only those were not the exact words heard by the chick sitting to the right of the respectable hen. You see, the neighboring chick was beginning to fall asleep. And in her sleepiness, what she heard was appalling. So as soon as the respectable hen fell asleep, the chattering chick began to spread the dreadful story: "Oh my dear," she clucked to the hen on her right, "I won't mention any names, but someone in this hen house plans on plucking out every one of her feathers, just because she thinks it will make her more beautiful!"

Above the hens in the hen house, a family of owls listened on in disgust. "What is the world coming to," Mother Owl hooted. And she flew across the road to spread the word. "One of the hens is plucking her feathers out one by one!" she screeched to her friend in the tree across the road.

"It can't be true!" The neighboring owl decided. "It's perfectly true, oo, oo, oo," Mother Owl hooted, "I heard it myself!"

Two pigeons listened to the owls and gasped. Immediately they flew off to the roster's perch. "It seems impossible, but three hens in the house across the street have plucked out all of their feathers. They stand naked tonight in the cool air!"

In the morning, the rooster rushed across the road. He flew into the hen's house and spoke to the most respectable hen. "I must tell you," he began, "in a farm far from here five hens have plucked out all of their feathers and frozen to death!" The respectable hen, of course, did not recognize her own story. She assured the rooster: "That's a most terrible story. I will call it in to the newspaper immediately. Then everyone in the county will know how disrespectful those hens behaved!"

And so the story was included in the next day's newspaper. And it is perfectly true—one little feather can easily become five hens!

Think and Discuss

What lesson does this story teach about gossip?

How can you help prevent gossip at your school?

Name _____

Considering Honesty

Answer the questions below concerning honesty based on your own value system.

1. What does it mean to live an honest life? _____
_____

2. What does it mean to be true to yourself? _____
_____

3. What does it mean to live a life of integrity? _____
_____

4. Do you consider it lying to mislead someone by leaving out important facts? Give an example.
_____
_____

5. Do you consider exaggeration dishonest? _____
_____

6. Plutarch said, "The very spring and root of honesty and virtue lie in good education." Do you think it is necessary to be educated in order to be honest?
_____
_____

0-7682-2795-X Character Education

Name _____

Honesty Log

Name _____

Character Trait	Example of a way I exhibited this trait	Example of a way I exhibited this trait
Truthfulness • telling the truth • stating accurate facts		
Trustworthiness • being reliable • being trusted		
Sincerity • showing true feelings • avoiding false impressions		
Honor • being true to my word • being worthy of respect		
Integrity • knowing what's right • adhering to my values		

Definition: _____

The most important trait is _____ because _____

_____

The least important trait is _____ because _____

_____

Encourage honesty, trustworthiness, and sincerity throughout the school year with these activities.

- Begin each day with a check-in procedure in which students share with the class some of their true emotions. Each student needs only to say one or two sentences and the exercise should be optional. An honest check-in response might sound something like this: "I had an argument with my sister on the bus this morning, and I am not in a very good mood. I will do my best to focus on schoolwork anyway."

- Establish a student court in which students are encouraged to settle playground and classroom disputes using honesty, fair judgement, and reasonable consequences. Be certain that such a court is monitored by an adult to ensure that there is no name-calling or finger pointing.

- Encourage students to develop trustworthiness by allowing them to grade their own papers and the papers of their classmates on occasion.

- Create a bulletin board entitled The Truth about Me onto which students can add images and words that symbolize their talents, hopes, dreams, and desires.

- The truth about a student who is not a "book learner" may be hidden in a class in which only paper and pencil tasks are assigned. A more rounded approach to teaching will allow the strengths of each of the students in your classroom to shine. Present lessons in a variety of formats and assign a multitude of tasks to accommodate everyone from hands-on to auditory to visual learners. If possible, provide students with learning style and multiple intelligence inventories to help them determine their true strengths.

Extension Activities

- Brainstorm slogans that will promote honesty in the classroom. Create buttons, posters, and banners displaying the slogans.

- Help shy students express themselves more fully through music, dance, and art.

- Require students to work in groups to research the lives of individuals who have sacrificed much for the sake of truth. Ask groups to present their findings to the rest of the class.

- Look for universal truths in proverbs, fables, and sayings from around the world. Interpret the stories and sayings with your class, and challenge your students to restate them in "kid terms."

- Invite a judge to speak to your class about truth in the courtroom. Alternatively, devise and send specific questions to a Supreme Court Justice.

- Watch and discuss movies whose themes involve truth and honesty.

- Challenge students to locate picture books involving the theme of honesty. Encourage them to read the stories to younger siblings or students from a younger class.

- Establish a "Sincere Student" prize to be awarded weekly to a student who demonstrates honesty in tangible ways. Students can nominate each other for the award based on specific situations they witness in the classroom, lunchroom, or playground.

- With your students, develop Twenty Reasons to Tell the Truth. Display your list in the classroom.

- Encourage your students to seek the truth in their studies and the world by thinking critically about things they read and hear.

Fairness

Note for Teachers:

This unit is designed to help fifth grade students learn about fairness and to encourage them to develop good character. The activities, which are tied to national language arts (NCTE) and social studies (NCSS) standards, help students explore several aspects of fairness through interactive writing, reading, and cooperative projects. Best of all, students will be introduced to the positive impact and value of being a fair person, while learning the importance of making positive choices for themselves.

Dear Parent or Guardian:

Our class is participating in a character-building unit of study on fairness. Together we will explore the many aspects of fairness and participate in a number of activities that aim to strengthen each student's understanding of fairness.

You are invited to share in your child's learning experience by continuing the process of teaching him or her about fairness at home. You can do this in several ways:

- Model fairness as you interact with others. Ask your child questions about fair play or share personal views with your child.

- Select a famous person you think demonstrates a strong sense of fairness. Talk about this person with your child. Tell or read stories that show how people demonstrate fairness through their actions and deeds.

- Discuss the ways family members are fair to each other in your home. Talk about your own family's experiences involving fairness.

- Set up "What Would You Do?" games. Use real or made-up situations to present your child with conflicts to work out. These games give children safe opportunities to practice making critical choices before they must make real-life choices.

- Help your child practice fairness in your own neighborhood.

These activities will empower your child to make positive choices and experience the impact and value of fairness firsthand. Your cooperation and assistance in reinforcing your child's education in good character is much appreciated.

Sincerely,

_____

Standards Correlation

English Language Arts Standards	Page Numbers
1. Read a wide range of texts.	53, 56, 58, 59, 60, 61, 68
2. Read a wide range of literature.	68
3. Apply a variety of strategies to comprehend and interpret texts.	57, 59, 60, 61
4. Use spoken, written, and visual language to communicate effectively.	53, 54, 55, 57, 58, 59, 60, 61, 62, 63, 64, 65, 66, 67, 69, 70
5. Use a variety of strategies while writing and use elements of the writing process to communicate.	60, 61, 71
6. Apply knowledge of language structure and conventions, media techniques, figurative language, and genre to create, critique, and discuss texts.	60, 61
7. Research issues and interests, pose questions, and gather data to communicate discoveries.	55, 64, 65, 66, 67
8. Work with a variety of technological and other resources to collect information and to communicate knowledge.	
9. Understand and respect the differences in language use across cultures, regions, and social roles.	
10. Students whose first language is not English use their first language to develop competencies in English and other content areas.	
11. Participate in a variety of literary communities.	
12. Use spoken, written, and visual language to accomplish purposes.	53, 54, 55, 57, 58, 59, 60, 61, 62, 63, 64, 65, 66, 67, 69, 70

Social Studies Standards	
1 . Culture: Compare similarities and differences between cultures. Describe the importance of cultural unity and diversity.	
2. Time, Continuity, and Change: Study people, places, and events of the past.	56, 57
3. People, Places, and Environments: Learn about geography and how people interact with the environment.	
4. Individual Development and Identity: Explore factors that contribute to one's personal identity.	53, 54, 55, 60, 61, 62, 63, 64, 65, 66, 67, 69, 70
5. Individuals, Groups, and Institutions: Identify and describe the roles and influences of various institutions.	56, 57, 60, 61, 64
6. Power, Authority, and Governance: Understand the purpose of government. Describe the rights and responsibilities of individuals and groups.	56, 57
7. Production, Distribution, and Consumption: Explore how people organize to produce, distribute, and consume goods and services.	
8. Science, Technology, and Society: Describe ways in which science and technology have changed lives.	
9. Global Connections: Investigate how world societies depend on one another.	
10. Civic Ideals and Practices: Recognize the functions and ideals of a democratic government. Explain the rights and responsibilities of citizens.	56, 57, 60, 61

Name _____

What Makes a Fair Person?

People appreciate and respect fair behavior from others, but sometimes people have different concepts of what the term really means. Here are just two possibilities:

People should all receive equal treatment.

Each person should get what he or she needs.

Directions: List two situations that relate to the somewhat conflicting definitions of fairness.

Just like people, each situation is different from another. It is important to consider each situation carefully before deciding how to handle it fairly. List two situations you have experienced in the last month that involved fairness. Describe each situation below.

People Should Receive Equal Treatment	**Everyone Gets What They Need**
If a girl and a boy do the same chores, they should receive the same allowance.	If one person has poor eyesight, he/she should be allowed to sit in the front of the classroom.
A. _____	A. _____
B. _____	B. _____

Situation One: _____

_____

Situation Two: _____

_____

Name _____

Identifying Behaviors

Brad is learning about fairness. What fair behaviors does he already use? What behaviors will he need to change?

Color the boxes that show fair behaviors GREEN.

Color the boxes of behaviors that need improvement RED.

A. Brad gets angry if someone disagrees with his ideas.

B. Brad raises his hand before speaking in class so that everyone can be heard.

H. Brad does all of his chores to help his family.

C. Brad only works well in groups when he gets to pick his partners.

G. Brad does his own schoolwork.

D. Brad only spreads rumors if he thinks they are true.

F. Brad lets his little brother watch television sometimes if there isn't something on that Brad would rather watch.

E. Brad keeps his promises.

For one of the boxes you colored red, explain how Brand can improve the behavior:

For box _____, Brad needs to _____

_____.

Name _____

Character in Action

Identify four fair behaviors demonstrated by your classmates.

Date: _____

I observed the following fair behavior: _____

_____

The result of this behavior was: _____

I felt this behavior was fair because: _____

Date: _____

I observed the following fair behavior: _____

_____

The result of this behavior was: _____

I felt this behavior was fair because: _____

Date: _____

I observed the following fair behavior: _____

_____

The result of this behavior was: _____

I felt this behavior was fair because: _____

Date: _____

I observed the following fair behavior: _____

_____

The result of this behavior was: _____

I felt this behavior was fair because: _____

Rosa Parks

Making the World a Better Place

Rosa Parks was a brave, young, African-American woman who helped make our country a fairer place for black citizens. In 1955, African-American people were required to give up their bus seats to white passengers. Even if the African-American passengers had boarded the buses before the white passengers, the African-American people were still supposed to get up and move to the back of the bus or stand in the aisle. That year, in Montgomery, Alabama, Rosa Parks decided to make her feelings known by refusing to move from her seat in the front of a bus so that a white passenger could sit down. Rosa was arrested because she was disobeying a city law by refusing to move for the white passenger.

Many Americans were very angry that Rosa had been arrested for standing up for what she felt was right and fair. People began to boycott city buses because they wanted to show support for Rosa's beliefs. This action cost the city of Montgomery money and angered many people. A Supreme Court Decision struck down the Montgomery city ordinance. After that decision, racial segregation was outlawed on all public means of transportation.

Thanks to Rosa Parks and many other brave Americans, African-Americans and other minority ethnic groups have won equal rights in many areas. If we all determine what is right and fair in our own minds and stand up for those beliefs, we can all help to make the world a better place.

Name _____

Rosa Parks

1. What unfair situation did Rosa Parks face?

   _____

   _____

2. How did Rosa Parks decide to express her beliefs?

   _____

   _____

3. What did Rosa hope to accomplish by her actions?

   _____

   _____

4. How did Rosa's behavior help make conditions more fair for the future?

   _____

   _____

5. Name and describe someone else whom you respect for bravely standing up for what he or she believed was right. This person may be someone you know personally or someone you have learned about in school.

   _____

   _____

   _____

   _____

   _____

   _____

   _____

   _____

   _____

   _____

Reader's Theater

A Difficult Decision

Roles to Assign:
> Narrator
> Shonda (age 10)
> Kelly (age 10—Shonda's friend)
> Stacey (age 9—Shonda's sister)
> Colby (age 18—Shonda and Stacey's brother)
> Mom (Shonda, Stacey, and Colby's mom)

Narrator: Shonda meets her friend, Kelly, in the school cafeteria.

Kelly: Hey, Shonda! I need to talk to you about something.

Shonda: What is it?

Kelly: I started dance lessons at that new studio in town, and it's so much fun! Will you tell your mom that you want to start lessons, too? I know you'll love it, and I bet we could be two of the best in the class.

Shonda: That does sound great, but I already have piano lessons on Tuesday afternoons. When do you have dance lessons?

Kelly: Class is on Monday and Wednesday nights at 6:30.

Shonda: Okay, terrific! I'll call you tonight and let you know.

Narrator: After school that day, Shonda spoke to her mom about the lessons. Stacey, Shonda's younger sister, is in the next room listening.

Shonda: Mom, I want to start dance lessons. Kelly has already started at the new studio down the street. The lessons are on Mondays and Wednesdays.

Mom: Well, you know your sister has soccer practice across town on Wednesday evenings, and we can't be two places at once. Besides, I'm not sure I can afford to pay tuition for dance lessons right now.

Shonda: Oh, Mom! I really want to be in dance classes with Kelly! Please?

Narrator: Stacey comes in from the next room.

Stacey: Shonda? I guess I could stop playing soccer for a while if you really want to go to dance lessons. Then we could probably afford to do it.

Shonda: But Stacey, you love soccer!

Stacey: Yes, but I could probably play again next season.

Shonda: Well . . . what do you think, Mom?

Mom: I think you need to make a fair decision on your own.

Shonda: Well, okay. I'll think about it.

Narrator: An hour later, Shonda calls her older brother, Colby, at college and tells him about the situation.

Shonda: . . . so, anyway, what do you think I should do, Colby? You know I've always loved music, and I'd really like to learn to dance.

Colby: Listen, Shonda. Mom told you it was up to you. My opinion is that you already have your piano lessons, you're doing well at piano, and you enjoy it. Stacey does well at soccer, and she enjoys that, too. It seems to me that she didn't have to offer to give up soccer, but she knew you would be unhappy if Mom couldn't afford to pay for both your lessons plus dance. Maybe you should think about your options, and consider how everyone will be affected by your decision.

Shonda: You're right, Colby. I knew talking to you would help. Thanks.

Narrator: Later that night Shonda goes downstairs to talk to her mom and her sister.

Shonda: Mom? Stacey? I just wanted to say thank you to both of you. Thanks, Stacey, for offering to give up soccer just for me, and thanks, Mom, for trusting me to make the right choice. I've decided I don't really need dance lessons right now. Maybe later I can take a break from piano and try dance for a while, but I don't want Stacey giving up something she loves. I'm sorry I wasn't thinking about everyone's feelings.

Mom: I'm proud of your decision, Shonda.

Shonda: I'm going to call Kelly.

How do you think Mom, Stacey, Colby, and Kelly will feel about Shonda's decision?

_____

_____

_____

Name _____

Write About It!

This Is Private!

Sometimes people need to know that what they say and do can be kept private. In fact, privacy is so important to people that our right to a certain amount of privacy is protected by the Constitution.

It is considered fair for a person to expect a certain amount of privacy. For example, if people choose to keep personal journals, or diaries, they expect other people not to read them without permission. On the lines below, write about a time when you have expected people to be fair by respecting your privacy.

_____

_____

_____

_____

There are times when the safety and well-being of others is more important than an individual's right to privacy. For example, it would not be fair for a student to bring a dangerous object to school, put it in a locker or backpack, and expect others to respect his or her privacy. If another student found out about the dangerous situation, it would fair, and important for that student to let a teacher or principal know about it. Everyone's safety would depend on that student's information.

Write about a time when privacy would not be a fair expectation. Explain why NOT keeping information private in that situation would be fairer for everyone involved.

_____

_____

_____

_____

_____

_____

_____

Name _____

The Fairness Dilemma

On the lines below, write a story about a fifth grade student who faces the decision of whether to keep something he has found for himself, or to try to locate the true owner.

Before you begin, jot down ideas for main characters, what might have been lost and found, doubts the main character might have about his decision, and how the story should be concluded. Remember to make fairness a priority.

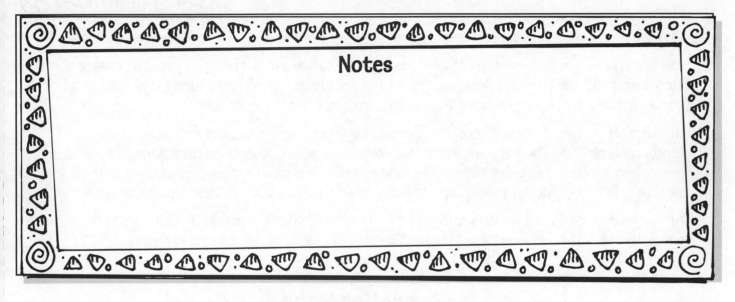

Notes

The Fairness Dilemma

_____

_____

_____

_____

_____

_____

_____

_____

_____

_____

_____

Role-Playing Activities

On the Spot

Teacher Note: Make a few copies of the resolution strips shown at the bottom of this page and on page 63.

1. Students will be divided into groups of three to four students each.

2. Give each group a resolution strip.

3. Allow all groups a few minutes to discuss the resolution strip. They will need to create a plot by identifying the conflict and sequencing events that lead to the resolution. This should all be done verbally among the group. Adjust the time needed if necessary.

4. At the end of the allowed discussion period, begin calling on groups to come to the front of the room and role-play for a minimum of two minutes each. Group members should read their resolution strip to the class before beginning the role-play. The role-play should portray the situation from beginning to end and should clearly lead to the fair resolution given on the strip.

5. At the end of class, have students comment either verbally or through journal writing about the two role-plays that showed the fairest, most logical ways of reaching the resolutions.

Resolution Strips

Resolution: Children decide that helping their father with the yardwork is a good way to help make more time for the family to spend together on weekends.

Resolution: A student decides that being the first one to say, "I'm sorry," when you are in an argument with your friend might be a way to make the friendship stronger.

Resolution: A mom decides that since her child has acted responsibly about her schoolwork, she will allow the child to decide on her own how much time to spend studying for her tests.

Role-Playing Activities

Resolution: A teacher decides to allow the class thirty minutes of free reading time each day if the students agree to tell the class about at least one book they have completed reading every two weeks.

Resolution: A child decides to put an advertisement in the newspaper for someone to adopt her dog because there is not enough time to pay attention to the dog.

Resolution: A mother decides that her older child may go to bed one hour later than her younger child because the older child spends more time doing homework that the younger child, and the older child doesn't seem to be as tired as the younger child in the evenings.

Resolution: Two children find a wallet outside of the community pool and decide to turn it in to the employees at the pool.

Resolution: A teacher decides to allow the students an extra day to study for their tests because there were severe storms during the previous week, and many people lost their electricity.

Resolution: A student hears that a friend of hers has been saying rude things about her to other people. She decides to ask the friend about the situation believing what she has heard.

Resolution: A student decides to tell the principal that he has heard other students teasing and threatening a child who is new to the school.

Resolution: A child decides to tell her mother that she was responsible for the broken window in the dining room even though the mother has no way of knowing how it happened.

0-7682-2795-X *Character Education*

Name _____

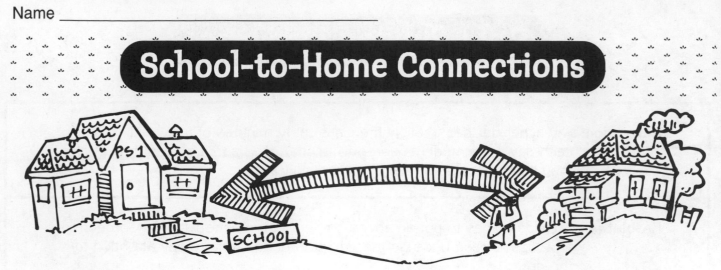

School-to-Home Connections

Homes are busy places! Even though our family members are among the most important people in our lives, fairness is sometimes overlooked at home. It is very important for family members to be able to depend on one another and to treat each other fairly.

Use the questions below to interview the people in your home about fairness. After writing down their responses, arrange a time to sit down with the whole family and share what you have learned. If everyone hears and understands each family member's feelings about fairness, a group effort can be made to make your home the fairest place it can be.

Interview Questions:

Family Member Interviewed: _____

1. What does the phrase "being fair with family" mean to you?

   _____

   _____

2. What are some things that we do as a family that involve fairness?

   _____

   _____

3. Do you think we share responsibilities fairly in our home? (Explain)

   _____

   _____

4. Do you think we consider each other's feelings fairly? (Explain)

   _____

   _____

5. Are there any actions that involve fairness where you think we should work on improvement?

   _____

   _____

Materials Needed:
- Copies of the student worksheet on page 66
- Copies of the task cards on page 67
- A large sheet of poster board or butcher paper for each group
- Markers

1. Divide your class into four groups and have them sit in different areas of the room.

2. Give each group a different task card from page 67, markers, and a large piece of poster board.

3. Give each student a worksheet. (page 66)

4. Explain to students that each group will be working on completing the task assigned to them in a fair manner. Tell students to use the worksheets to help organize and distribute responsibilities fairly.

5. Once all students have completed the worksheets by discussing the task with their groups, each student should take turns filling in the following information on the poster board. (You may want to have the students go around their groups clockwise, filling in one procedure at a time on the poster so that all students participate in the final product.)

Poster

Task to be achieved: _____

_____

Procedures for achieving the task (in order):

_____

_____

_____

_____

_____

_____

_____

After all groups have completed a poster, have the groups share their posters with the class.

Name _____

The Task at Hand

1. What is the assigned task?

   _____

2. What procedures will be necessary to carry out the task?

   A. _____ ☐

   B. _____ ☐

   C. _____ ☐

   D. _____ ☐

   E. _____ ☐

3. Which group member will complete each procedure?

   Procedure A: _____ ☐

   Procedure B: _____ ☐

   Procedure C: _____ ☐

   Procedure D: _____ ☐

   Procedure E: _____ ☐

4. In the boxes next to each procedure, write the number to tell which procedure needs to be completed first, second, third, etc.

   For example: Getting the needed materials ☐

Cooperative Learning

Task Cards

Task 1:
Create a room that is completely safe for toddlers.

Task 2:
Create an animal-friendly zoo.

Task 3:
Create an entertaining and educational school assembly.

Task 4:
Create the most student-friendly school desk possible.

0-7682-2795-X *Character Education*

The Lion and the Mouse

Once when a Lion was asleep, a little Mouse began running up and down on top of him. This soon wakened the Lion, who placed his huge paw upon the little Mouse and opened his big jaws to swallow him.

"Pardon, O King," cried the little Mouse, "let me go this time and I shall never forget it. Who knows but what I may be able to do you a good turn one of these days?"

The Lion was so tickled at the idea of the Mouse being able to help him that he lifted up his paw and let the Mouse go.

Some time later the Lion was caught in a trap. The hunters, who wanted to carry him alive to the King, tied him to a tree while they went in search of a wagon. Just then the little Mouse happened to pass by and, seeing the sad plight in which the Lion was, went up to him and soon gnawed away the ropes that bound the King of Beasts.

"Was I not right?" said the little Mouse.

Little friends may prove great friends.

Thinking about the selection:

What would probably have happened to the lion if he had not decided to let the mouse go free?

_____

_____

_____

Draw and color a picture of a scene from the fable that you might use if you were the illustrator.

Name _____

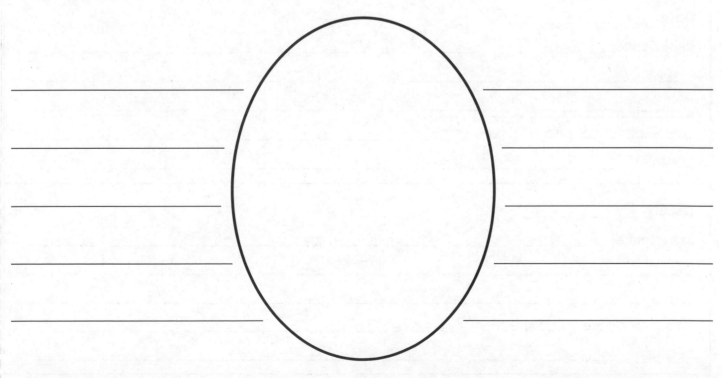

1. What is your own personal definition of fairness?

   Fairness means_____

   _____

   _____

2. Has your opinion about treating people fairly changed since you started this unit on fairness?

   Circle one: yes   no

   Explain your thoughts _____

   _____

   _____

3. I think I am a fair person because _____

   _____

   _____

Draw a picture of yourself in the circle below. On the lines coming out of the circle, list qualities about your character, or personality, that you are proud of! This graphic could be improved upon or it could be used.

Name _____

My Journal Log

This is a log for you to record times when you have made a special effort to be fair to others. It can also be used to acknowledge how much you have appreciated someone else's fairness to you. Whenever you experience a situation involving fairness, write a journal entry on this page.

For example:

Date: September 1st

Experience: I made a special effort to be fair today by letting my little sister watch her favorite television show even though it is not one that I like to watch.

This experience made me feel good because it made my sister happy, and she knew that I cared about her.

Date: _____

Experience: _____

_____

_____

This experience made me feel _____

because _____.

Date: _____

Experience: _____

_____

_____

This experience made me feel _____

because _____.

Date: _____

Experience: _____

_____

_____

This experience made me feel _____

because _____.

Extension Activities

The following projects may be used to help students apply the concept of fairness in their lives both inside and outside of the classroom.

Share a Story:

Objective:

The students will use the writing process to create a fable relating to fairness and read it aloud to a younger student, friend, or relative.

1. Read a fable relating to fairness aloud to the students. One example is "The Lion and the Mouse" on page 68.

2. Explain to students that they will be writing fables of their own that have the theme of fairness.

3. **Prewriting:** Have the students answer the following questions to build characters, settings and plots for their fables.

   Who?

   When?

   Where?

   What?

   Why?

   How?

   Reinforce the idea of fairness as a theme for the stories.

4. **Rough Draft:** Have students use their prewriting to form organized paragraphs.

5. **Revision:** Have students read their fables in partners, giving each other suggestions for making the meaning clearer.

6. **Editing:** Have students check their papers carefully for errors in spelling and/or punctuation.

7. **Final Copy:** Have students fold several sheets of paper in half to create a book. The fable should be copied into the booklet in ink, leaving every other page blank to add in illustrations.

8. **Publishing:** Allow students to share their fables with younger class or encourage them to read the fables to younger children. Align copy for this list.

Extension Activities

Recognition Receptacle

Objective:
Students will demonstrate an understanding of fairness by noting their observations of classmates behaving fairly and rewarding that behavior by submitting awards to the "receptacle."

Materials Needed:
- A medium-sized box
- Copies of the award certificates on this page plus copy of page 55

1. Explain to students that they will be given one week to identify at least three behaviors of fairness demonstrated by other classmates.

2. When a student observes a fair behavior, the following directions should be followed:

   The student should complete an award certificate and place it in the Recognition Receptacle.

   The student should complete a journal entry on the "character in action" page describing the fair behavior. When journal entries are completed, the student submits the journal to the teacher.

During this assignment's duration, the teacher should check the receptacle daily for submissions and hand the awards out to the students being recognized. The awards will not have the names of the students who have submitted them unless those students wish to add their names.

Date _____

In Recognition of :

_____

for demonstrating fairness by :

_____

_____

You Are Appreciated!!!

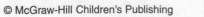

Dear Teacher:

As a teacher, it is likely that one of your goals is to help your students to become more responsible in their own choices and to behave in a responsible manner in all of their surroundings. The activities in this unit will help you with exactly that! Lessons are included which define responsible behavior on an age-appropriate level. Students will be encouraged to see reliable behavior in those around them. They will also be encouraged to become more responsible for their own actions.

A variety of formats are included to interest even the most reluctant learner. Many of the lessons are tied to English and Social Studies standards that will enable you to cover important skills while teaching good character development. Emphasis is placed on real-life situations easily identified by your fifth graders. An interesting biography on Theodore Roosevelt introduces a hard-working person from the past who found that being responsible changed his country.

The answer to the question on page 76 is "YOU'RE RIGHT."

Dear Parents and Caregivers:

How many times have you wished that your child would take more responsibility in the home? How many times have you wished that your child would act more responsibly outside of the home, too? As a teacher, I share those same desires. Our class is about to begin a unit of study that should help us both. We will be working through a series of activities about becoming more responsible people.

I encourage you to ask your child about our activities. We will be completing written assignments, engaging in role-playing activities, participating in classroom discussions and projects, playing a game, and engaging in other activities as well. The aim of all of these activities is to increase your child's sense of responsibility. I will be sending some of the activities home so that you may discuss them with your child.

Please remember to give your students clear, manageable tasks at home to complete on a regular basis. And please contact me if you have any questions about this important area of study.

Sincerely,

_____

English Language Arts Standards	Page Numbers
1. Read a wide range of texts.	75, 78, 90, 93, 94
2. Read a wide range of literature.	78, 79, 80, 81, 93, 94
3. Apply a variety of strategies to comprehend and interpret texts.	78, 79, 80, 81, 90
4. Use spoken, written, and visual language to communicate effectively.	78, 79, 80, 81, 93, 94
5. Use a variety of strategies while writing and use elements of the writing process to communicate.	80, 81, 93, 94
6. Apply knowledge of language structure and conventions, media techniques, figurative language, and genre to create, critique, and discuss texts.	80, 81, 90, 93, 94
7. Research issues and interests, pose questions, and gather data to communicate discoveries.	78, 79, 90, 93, 94
8. Work with a variety of technological and other resources to collect information and to communicate knowledge.	78, 79, 90, 93, 94
9. Understand and respect the differences in language use across cultures, regions, and social roles.	80, 81
10. Students whose first language is not English use their first language to develop competencies in English and other content areas.	
11. Participate in a variety of literary communities.	78, 79, 90, 93, 94
12. Use spoken, written, and visual language to accomplish purposes.	76, 77, 78, 79, 80, 81, 82, 83, 84, 85, 86, 93, 94
Social Studies Standards	
1. Culture: Compare similarities and differences between cultures. Describe the importance of cultural unity and diversity.	80, 81, 83
2. Time, Continuity, and Change: Study people, places, and events of the past.	78, 79, 83, 86, 93, 94
3. People, Places, and Environments: Learn about geography and how people interact with the environment.	83
4. Individual Development and Identity: Explore factors that contribute to one's personal identity.	82, 84, 85, 86, 93, 94
5. Individuals, Groups, and Institutions: Identify and describe the roles and influences of various institutions.	78, 79, 93, 94
6. Power, Authority, and Governance: Understand the purpose of government. Describe the rights and responsibilities of individuals and groups.	82, 93, 94
7. Production, Distribution, and Consumption: Explore how people organize to produce, distribute, and consume goods and services.	
8. Science, Technology, and Society: Describe ways in which science and technology have changed lives.	83
9. Global Connections: Investigate how world societies depend on one another.	
10. Civic Ideals and Practices: Recognize the functions and ideals of a democratic government. Explain the rights and responsibilities of citizens.	82, 90, 93, 94

Name _____

What Is Responsibility?

Responsibility is doing what is expected of you. It is taking care of the things that have been put in your care. If you are a *responsible* person, other people know they can count on you to follow through on what you start. They know you will do what you've agreed to do. When children are very young, they act responsibly because they don't want to get into trouble. As they grow older, they begin to act responsibly because they know it's the right thing to do, even when others aren't looking.

Responsibility can also mean *blame*. If your dad's car breaks down, he will try to figure out which car part is *responsible* for the problem. In the same way, if the teacher walks into the room and finds her flower vase broken and on the floor, she may ask, "Who is *responsible* for this?"

A *responsibility* can be something for which you have been left in charge. For example, at home you may have *responsibility* for keeping your room clean. At school, you may be asked take *responsibility* for the classroom pet.

Here are more examples of how some students show responsibility:

Evan is on time for school.

Jen writes "thank you notes" for gifts she receives.

Sal returns phone calls.

Gretta clears her dishes and puts food away after she has a snack.

Alice wipes up milk if she spills it.

List three more ways in which you can show responsibility at home:

1. _____

2. _____

3. _____

List four more ways in which you can show responsibility at school:

1. _____

2. _____

3. _____

4. _____

Name _____

Responsibility Quiz

Take this quiz to see if you can identify responsible behavior. Circle the letter in front of the best answer(s). Be ready to discuss your answers with your classmates.

1. When using a computer in the classroom, a responsible student would
   A. take as much time as possible on the computer.
   G. complete one task on the computer and then get off to allow others to use it.
   E. open a lot of programs and change a lot of settings.

2. When watching younger brothers and sisters, a responsible babysitter would
   Y. keep a close eye on the children in order to be sure they are safe and content.
   E. take the opportunity to make long phone calls to friends.
   S. not allow the kids to move off the sofa.

3. Anyone who wants to be responsible to keep his neighborhood clean and tidy would
   E. pick up any litter he sees along the sidewalk and roadway.
   A. pick up trash only in front of his own house.
   T. be sure that bushes are trimmed, snow is shoveled, and leaves are raked on his own property.

4. As part of a family concerned about the cost of energy, a responsible person would
   B. leave appliances and lights on when not in use.
   U. turn off lights when he leaves a room.
   G. run the air conditioner as much as possible to be sure it's working properly.

5. A fifth grader who wants to learn good habits that will help him later in life would
   H. turn in assignments on time.
   I. help the teacher with any chores that she requests.
   S. do his work whenever it's convenient.

6. A person who wants to behave responsibly in his country would
   O. vote in elections.
   U. avoid paying all taxes.
   R. stay informed on important issues.

7. A responsible worker would
   R. do his best work all the time.
   U. work hard only when the boss is looking.
   G. come late to meetings.

To find out if you have the right answers, write the letters you circled on the corresponding blanks. For questions that have more than one right answer, you'll have to decide which letter makes the most sense for each blank.

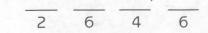

<u> </u> <u> </u> <u> </u>' <u> </u> <u> </u>   <u> </u> <u> </u> <u> </u> <u> </u> <u> </u>
2   6   4   6   3   7   5   1   5   3

(Teacher: See p. 73)

76   0-7682-2795-X *Character Education*

Name _____

Real-Life Responsibility

You have seen many people act responsibly throughout your life. Think about examples of responsible behavior that you have witnessed. Complete each set of binoculars below. In the blank space, write a sentence about an example of responsible behavior that you have seen.

Example from your classroom: _____

Example from your home: _____

Example from your neighborhood: _____

0-7682-2795-X *Character Education*

Theodore Roosevelt

Theodore Roosevelt was born on October 27, 1858 in New York City. His parents were wealthy, so in some ways life was very easy for him. But Theodore was a sickly child. He had asthma and was also near-sighted. He had to work very hard to become strong physically.

In 1878, Theodore's father died, and T.R. decided he needed to work and earn a living. He said, "I had enough bread. What I had to do was to provide the butter and jam." T.R. decided to take responsibility for his own future. Theodore graduated from Harvard University in 1880. He was married in the same year to Alice Lee. Sadly, she died just four years later. After her death, Theodore moved to North Dakota to live as a rancher. While there, doctors told him he had a weak heart. So T.R. pushed himself physically. He climbed mountains, tended cattle, and helped capture bandits. Two years later, he returned to the East, and then he married Edith Carow. Altogether, Roosevelt had six children. He planned picnics, camping trips, and fun holiday celebrations with his family.

Roosevelt became involved in politics shortly after his father's death. He joined a political club in New York that was known for being dishonest. T.R. quickly tried to clean it up, and he became known as someone who fought for change. When he was just 23 years old, Roosevelt was elected to the New York State Assembly.

In 1897, President McKinley appointed Roosevelt to be the assistant secretary of the Navy. He was concerned there would be a war with Spain. When war was finally declared, T.R. resigned from his Navy position to command a group of volunteer cavalry men that he himself had organized. This group was known as "The Rough Riders."

Because of his success in the war, Roosevelt was elected governor of New York in 1898. In this job, he again fought for honesty in government. He made important changes to improve the lives of people in New York. Roosevelt became very popular throughout the nation. In 1900, he was elected vice-president with McKinley at the Republican convention. When McKinley was assassinated, Roosevelt became President of the United States. He took the oath of office on September 14, 1901.

As president, Roosevelt shouldered the responsibility for many problems in government and around the world, and he worked to correct them. He worked to make big business less powerful. He worked for conservation projects and added millions of acres to the national forests. He helped pass a Food and Drug Act that insured safer foods. He helped to speed up completion of the Panama Canal. He even won the Nobel Peace Prize for negotiating a peace treaty between Russia and Japan. Theodore served as President of the United States until March 3, 1909. On January 6, 1919, Theodore Roosevelt died in his New York home. He left behind the record of a very responsible leader.

Name _____

Think and Discuss:

1. How did Theodore Roosevelt take responsibility for his health?

   _____

   _____

2. Explain what Roosevelt meant by this statement: "I had enough bread. What I had to do was to provide the butter and jam."

   _____

   _____

3. How do you know that Roosevelt was a responsible father?

   _____

   _____

4. How did the behavior of Roosevelt change the government of his city, state, and country?

   _____

   _____

5. Roosevelt was not responsible for many of the problems he encountered. Yet he acted responsibly in trying to solve them. What problems around you can you try to solve?

   _____

   _____

   _____

Dig Deeper!

Choose one of the following:

1. Use internet resources to learn more about the Rough Riders and Roosevelt's leadership in this group. Write a one-page report about this volunteer cavalry.

2. Theodore Roosevelt was known by "T.R." and another well-known nickname. Can you find out what it was? How did the nickname become so popular, and how is it still used today? Use internet resources or reference books to help you.

3. President Roosevelt's program was called, "The Square Deal." Find the four main points of this famous program.

The Little Red Hen

Setting: *A fifth grade classroom*

Characters: *The teacher, Mr. Thomas; students Aaron, Beth, Charlotte, Devin, and Stevie*

Mr. Thomas: Okay, class, you know that we all voted to have a class play. We decided to do this for the younger students in our school, if you remember, and also for another reason. We said that we would perform for our families and the community. We'd charge an admission price and then use that money for a new classroom computer. Let me remind you that we all agreed we would work together and do our share.

All students (*speaking at the same time*): Yes, that's right, Mr. Thomas. We agree. You're exactly right!

Mr. Thomas: I found a great version of the old children's story, *The Little Red Hen*, that's written as a play. How many of you remember that tale?

All students quickly raise their hands.

Mr. Thomas: Now, kids, we need to cover a lot of different jobs here. Who will be in charge of designing the scenery?

Aaron: Not me. I can't draw.

Beth: Not me. I don't have time.

Charlotte: Not me. I don't like to get messy.

Devin: Not me. I hate art.

Stevie: I'll do it, Mr. Thomas. I want to help!

Mr. Thomas: Thank you, Stevie. Okay, now who will design and type the programs?

Aaron: Not me. I can't type.

Beth: Not me. I'm too busy.

Charlotte: Not me. I don't like that sort of thing.

Devin: Not me. I hate to type.

Stevie: I'll do it, Mr. Thomas. I want to help!

Mr. Thomas: Thanks, again, Stevie! Are you sure you can handle all of this? *(Stevie nods "yes" with his head.)* Next, we need people to act out the parts.

Aaron: Not me. I can't act.

Beth: Not me. I don't have time to learn the lines.

Charlotte: Not me. I don't like memorizing.

Devin: Not me. I hate acting!

Stevie: I'll do it, Mr. Thomas. I want to help!

Mr. Thomas: *(taking a deep breath)* Okay, guys. When it's time to use that new computer in this classroom, this is how it's going to be. Aaron, I'm assuming that you won't know how. Beth, I'm assuming you won't have time. Charlotte, I'm assuming that you won't like using the computer, and Devin, I'm assuming that you hate computers. I'm also figuring that Stevie will want to, and unless some things change quickly, he'll be the only one that's allowed to use it!

Aaron, Beth, Charlotte, and Devin: *speaking at the same time, phrases such as:* Awe, c'mon, Mr. Thomas. That's not fair. Why should Stevie have all the fun?

Think and Discuss

1. Why do you think Mr. Thomas said that only Stevie could use the new computer?

2. If possible, find a copy of *The Little Red Hen* and read it together. You'll see how the skit above matches its theme. Consider rewriting *The Little Red Hen* as a classroom play and performing it for younger students in your school.

3. Aaron, Beth, Charlotte and Devin all had reasons for not doing any of the things Mr. Thomas asked. Do you think their reasons were valid? When is it okay to say "no" to someone's requests? When is saying "no" and giving a "reason" really just making an excuse?

Name _____

John D. Rockefeller said, "I believe that every right implies a responsibility . . ." In other words, he felt that for every right or privilege someone has, he also has a responsibility.

Consider this example. When you one day earn the *right* to drive your parents' car, you will also have a responsibility to drive safely. You and your parents must also be sure you have auto insurance. What other responsibilities will you have as a driver?

Listed below in the left column are more rights that you have already or that you may have in the future. Opposite each right, list the responsibilities that go with that right.

Rights	**Responsibilities**
1. right to attend school	_____ _____ _____
2. right to own clothes, toys and other possessions	_____ _____ _____
3. right to use the classroom computer	_____ _____ _____
4. right to freedom of speech	_____ _____ _____

Name _____

Rights and Responsibilities

You probably already know many of the responsibilities that you and your parents have every day, every week, and every year. But do you know how those responsibilities might change if you lived in another culture? For each culture listed below, write responsibilities you might have that are the same as the ones you have now. Then list responsibilities that are different. Some examples are filled in for you.

Time and Place	Same Responsibilities	Different Responsibilities
Living in America in a log cabin in the 1800's	washing dishes setting the table,	carrying water in from the creek, cutting firewood,
Living in a palace in England in 1920		learn proper etiquette as an obligation of royalty,
Living in Russia in 1950		
Living in California in 2050		

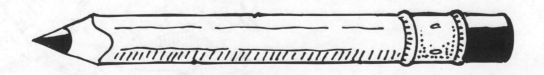

 0-7682-2795-X *Character Education*

Do you know how to be a responsible person? Are you ready to help others learn, too? Read each situation below. Then pair up with another student or students and act out two of the following scenarios. Show how you can encourage each other to become more responsible.

Mrs. Jones is giving away free kittens, and she wants to be sure the kittens go to good homes. Michelle really wants one of the kittens, but her father thinks Michelle won't be responsible enough to take good care of the kitten. Should Michelle's dad let her take one of the kittens? Should Mrs. Jones give one to Michelle? Act out the parts of Mrs. Jones, Michelle, and Michelle's father.

Alex told Brenda that Julie was grounded by her parents for two weeks because she lied to them. Brenda knows that Julie sometimes lies, but she doesn't know if Alex has his facts straight this time. She knows that he sometimes likes to gossip whether or not he knows what he's saying is true. Brenda would like to tell her best friend Meg, but she's not sure if she should or not. Role-play the parts of Alex and Brenda. Add the parts of Meg and Julie if necessary..

Rosa and Marcie want to go to the store to look at CDs. Their mother gives them permission, and she asks them to take Pedro, their little brother, with them. Mother asks them to "be responsible" for Pedro and make sure he behaves. While at the store, Pedro accidentally knocks over a small statue and breaks it. Rosa sees this happen. Marcie and the store's owner do not see it. Should Rosa tell Marcie and the store's owner? If she tells, will she and Marcie have to pay for it themselves, since they were told to be responsible for their little brother? Act out the parts of Rosa, Marcie, Pedro, their mother, and the store owner.

Audrey is folding the laundry. Her friend Sabrina phones and invites her over for a party later that evening. The two friends end up talking a long time. Then it's time for dinner. Audrey's parents agree that she may go to Sabrina's party if her chores are done in time. Sabrina rings the doorbell just as Audrey finishes her meal. The laundry is still sitting in the living room. What should the girls do? Act out the parts of Audrey, Sabrina, and Audrey's parents.

0-7682-2795-X *Character Education*

Tom and Mike are at the football game. Mike's older sister Shanna and her boyfriend Perry are supposed to give Tom and Mike a ride home in Shanna's car. After the football game, the five of them walk to the car. Tom and Mike can tell that Perry has been drinking alcohol. Shanna hands her car keys to Perry. What should Mike and Tom do? Act out the roles of Tom, Mike, Shanna, and Perry.

In the summer, Mark and Molly were very excited about starting a garden. They wanted to plant a lot of vegetables. Now it's time to hoe the corn and pick the beans. They are not so interested in the garden now, but their parents think they should help. Act out the parts of Mark, Molly, and their parents.

Mrs. Fisher's fifth grade class is going to have a bake sale. The class decided they would all work together to raise money for the local homeless shelter. Bryce and Betsy only want to work on selling the goods, but Mrs. Fisher thinks that since they are very good in art, they should work on designing the posters and ads instead. Bryce and Betsy go to their friend Keith and ask for advice. What should he tell them? Act out the parts of Mrs. Fisher, Bryce, Betsy, and Keith.

Hal and Jed Simmons are at the mall with their parents. Mrs. Simmons is in a wheelchair and must be pushed. Mr. Simmons decides to leave the mall briefly to put some packages in the car. He asks the boys to "be responsible" for their mother. While Mr. Simmons is away, Hal suggests they wheel their mom down to the video store so that the boys can browse there. Jed knows that the store is very small and crowded and that there's no room inside for the wheelchair. If they go inside that store, they will need to leave their mom outside the store by herself. What should Jed suggest? Role-play the parts of Hal, Jed, Mr. Simmons and Mrs. Simmons.

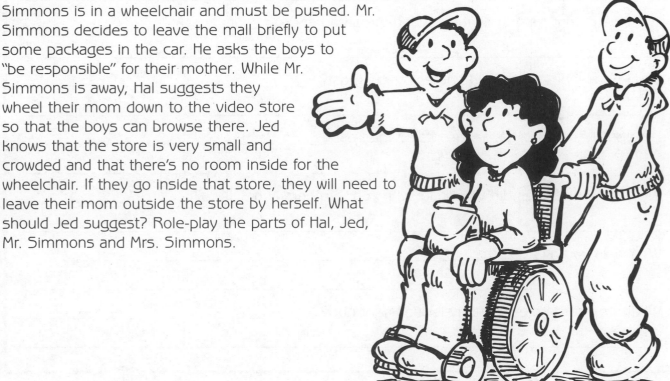

Name _____

School-to-Home Connection

You have been learning about how you can be a responsible member of your family, school, and community. Now it's time to think about how someone else has been responsible in the past. Contact one of your grandparents, great-grandparents, aunts, or uncles. Interview that person using the questions below. Record their answers and share their remarks with other members of your family.

Interview Questions

1. Where did you live when you were my age?_____
_____

2. What other people were in your family?_____
_____

3. What were your responsibilities at home during the school year? _____
_____

4. What were your responsibilities during the summer? _____
_____

5. What household chores did you enjoy the most? _____
_____

6. Did you like working inside or outside the best? _____
_____

7. What responsibilities did you share with your brothers and sisters? _____
_____

8. What was your first job? _____
_____

9. What are your biggest responsibilities right now? _____
_____

Responsibility Charades

Students will love acting out responsible (and irresponsible) roles with this fun-filled game. In charades, a team member tries to show a specific action to other team members. If the team guesses correctly, they score. If they don't, the other team gets a chance to score. Here are all the details:

1. Decide whether the students will act their charades alone or in pairs. Photocopy either page 88 (solo actors) or page 89 (pairs of actors) and cut apart the actions. Fold each slip of paper in half and place in a large paper bag or hat.

2. In this game, all actions can be divided into these categories:

   • Responsible behavior at home

   • Responsible behavior at school

   • Responsible behavior in the community

   • Irresponsible behavior

   Before you begin the play, the entire class should agree on the actions that will be used to designate each category. For example, they might decide that for the "responsible behavior at home" category, they will put their fingertips together to show a roof top.

3. Divide the class into two teams. Be sure that team members rotate so that everyone gets a turn to "act."

4. The first player on Team 1 draws a slip of paper. That person reads the action to be displayed and decides into which of the categories it fits.(Some actions may fit into more than one.) The actor gives the paper to the teacher who acts as judge. The player then indicates which of the four categories apply. The player then demonstrates the action and is not allowed to speak. A time limit of 30–60 seconds should be set for acting and guessing. If the team guesses the action correctly in time, they score one point. (The judge may decide if the guess counts when it is similar to, but not exactly the same as, the words on the paper.) If Team 1 does not guess correctly, then Team 2 can guess. If Team 2 guesses correctly, they score one point. If neither team is correct, a new slip of paper is drawn by the next player on Team 1.

5. Team 2 then sends its first player to draw a slip of paper and play continues as above.

6. The team with the most points at the end of the time period is the winning team.

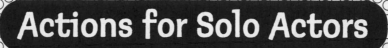

washing and drying dishes	straightening books on the shelves
vacuuming the floor	picking up litter
walking the dog	cleaning the chalkboard
setting the table	erasing an answer and writing it again neatly
mowing the lawn	spilling your milk and cleaning it up
shoveling snow	watering plants
making a bed	pulling weeds and hoeing in the garden or park
writing a letter to a friend and mailing it	breaking something and hiding the evidence
raking leaves	dumping out the trash can without cleaning it up
washing dirty windows	playing the drums and making a lot of noise
passing out papers for the teacher	riding a bike recklessly and without a helmet

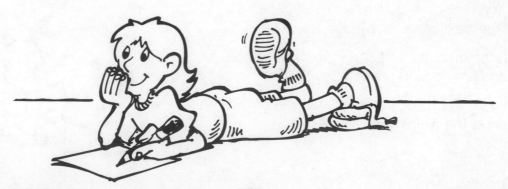

   0-7682-2795-X *Character Education*

Actions for Pairs of Actors

playing ball with a younger sibling	helping someone wash the car
helping someone who just fell and was hurt	folding large bed sheets
helping one of your parents carry groceries in from the car	swimming with a buddy
helping another student with math problems	taking turns on the playground slide
helping a senior citizen cross the street	performing a puppet show for kids at the library
breaking something and then telling the teacher you did it	practicing the piano when your friend wants you to go out and play
being late for an appointment with a friend	slamming the door in a friend's face and walking away mad
blaming someone else for something you did	talking with a friend too long on the phone
twirling a jumprope for other children	bullying other kids on the playground

0-7682-2795-X *Character Education*

Responsible Quotations

Read these quotations made by famous people about responsibility.

> You can't evade the responsibility of tomorrow by evading it today.
> —Abraham Lincoln

> Responsibilities gravitate to the person who can shoulder them.
> —Elbert Hubbard

> Responsibility is the price of greatness.
> ---Winston Churchill

> Every man must carry his own sack to the mill.
> ---Italian proverb

> If each one sweeps before his own door, the whole street is clean.
> —Yiddish proverb

> The first requisite of a good citizen in this republic of ours is that he should be able and willing to pull his weight.
> —Theodore Roosevelt

> Everyone ought to bear patiently the results of his own conduct.
> —Phaedrus

Work with a partner to complete these activities:

1. Look up the meaning of any words that are new to you.

2. Individually select your favorite quotation. Tell your partner why you like it best.

3. Research the person or the quotation. Use the Internet or an encyclopedia.

4. Choose another quotation together. Discuss what it means when you apply it to your own lives at home, at school, and in your community.

5. Work together to make a poster that contains the words of one of the quotations. Add your own illustrations.

 0-7682-2795-X *Character Education*

Name _____

How Responsible Am I?

Take this quiz to see how responsible you are. For each sentence, give yourself one of these numbers:

1 = I don't usually display this behavior.

2 = Sometimes I do this.

3 = I almost always behave in this manner.

_____ A. I am on time for school and other events.

_____ B. I do my chores at home.

_____ C. I do the jobs at school that the teacher gives me.

_____ D. When I do a job, I try to do it well.

_____ E. I follow safety rules.

_____ F. I do not blame others when I make a bad choice.

_____ G. I do not ask others to make poor choices.

_____ H. When others try to pressure me to do the wrong thing, I make my own right choice.

_____ I. I am a responsible member of my planet. I do not litter or waste resources.

_____ J. I take good care of the things that are placed under my care.

_____ K. When I see other people doing unsafe things, I tell an adult.

1. Now add your points. The highest score is 36. If you have at least 24 points, you are becoming a responsible person.

2. On the back of this page, write three more sentences that describe responsible actions. Score yourself on these, too.

3. Save this page. In a few months, score yourself again. Hopefully you will score even higher!

Name _____

Now that you have learned about being a responsible person, fill in the blanks to complete this pledge.

Responsibility Pledge

On this date _____, I hereby pledge

to do my best to be a responsible citizen in:
(check all that you agree with)

☐ my home

☐ my classroom

☐ my school

☐ my community

☐ my country

☐ my world

Even when others do not behave responsibly,

even when others make fun of me,

even when _____,

even when _____,

I will still be a responsible person.

Signed,

_____
Name

Give your students opportunities to become increasingly responsible throughout the school year with these extension activities.

- Set up an imaginary community to help your students learn about the many responsibilities that must be fulfilled for a community to function well. Begin by listing all the roles that exist in the community. Then, have each student select one job of interest. Next, ask each student to learn about the specific duties of that job and any skills and education needed to perform those duties. Then, gather together and ask students to share their findings with the class. Finally, talk about the roles that were missing and how that would affect a real community. For example, if no one signed up to be a firefighter, or a doctor, or a sanitation worker, how would the community be affected? Help students to see the interdependence all citizens have with one another.

- Here's an activity that parents will love! Ask students to make a Housekeeping Responsibilities chart to take home. The chart should contain about ten lines and three columns. On the lines, each student should list the jobs required to keep a tidy room. Household tasks include washing and drying clothes, cleaning bathrooms, dusting, and taking out the trash. The columns should be labeled Daily, Weekly, and Monthly. Ask each student to put a small x in one column for each task to show how often he believes each task needs to be completed. Then ask students to take the charts home to review with their family. After any needed adjustments are made, family members can write the name of the person assigned to each of these chores for the next month.

- Help students learn about the influence of responsible people in their lives. First ask students to list three sentences that describe their strengths, likes/dislikes, and hobbies. Ask them if anyone in their family or group of friends could write those same sentences about themselves. Help students to see the influence these important people have made on their lives. Then instruct students to write a paragraph about how one person in their family has been responsible for influencing them.

- Organize your students into Responsibility Teams. Place four or five students on each team. Ask each team to study a different question and then propose projects that answer it. Here are possible questions to assign to your teams:

    How can we make our classroom better?

    How can we make our school better?

    How we can encourage other kids our age to become more responsible?

    How can we act more responsibly in our community?

Each team should try to think of ten ideas in response to their question. They then discuss the pros and cons of each one. Next, they should narrow their list of ideas down to their top three choices. Then, each team should present their top three ideas and discuss them with the entire class. Let the class vote to decide which project it will do. The class then needs to decide what committees will need to be formed to plan the details of the project and carry it out.

- Arrange students in small groups according the types of pets they own (or would like to own). For example, all the cat owners could be in the same group. Next, ask them to list the main responsibilities of owning their type of pet. Finally, ask each group to produce a small "infomercial" to perform for the class that would explain their responsibilities as pet owners. Students may want to mention specific foods, toys, or other products that they recommend.

- After studying the biography of President Theodore Roosevelt on page 78, challenge your students to learn how other past national and international leaders have taken responsibility for solving important problems. Encourage students to search online sources and reference books to learn how former presidents acted responsibly as private citizens. Assign one leader of the past to a small group of students. Ask each group to share their findings in a poster or wall chart.

- Ask students to conduct internet searches for the word *responsibility*. What information and activities can they find? Using a thesaurus, what synonyms can they locate for responsibility?

- Begin a classroom "Responsibility in Action" poster. Ask students to be on the lookout for responsible behavior in their lives, in books they read, on television, and in movies. When they see responsible behavior, they may jot down a sentence or two describing it on the poster. They may also add a small sketch if they wish.

Cooperation

Note for Teachers:

This unit is designed to help fifth grade students learn about cooperation and encourage them to develop good character. The activities, which are tied to national language arts (NCTE) and social studies (NCSS) standards, help students explore several aspects of cooperation through interactive writing, reading, and cooperative projects. Best of all, students will be introduced to the positive impact and value of being a cooperative person, while learning the importance of making positive choices for themselves.

Dear Parent or Guardian:

Our class is participating in a character-building unit of study on cooperation. Together we will explore the many aspects of cooperation and participate in a number of activities that aim to strengthen each student's understanding of cooperation.

You are invited to share in your child's learning experience by continuing the process of teaching him or her about cooperation at home. You can do this in several ways:

- Model cooperation as you interact with others. Ask your child questions about being cooperative and share your own views of its importance with your child.

- Select a famous person you think represents a living example of someone who demonstrated the importance of cooperation. Talk about this person with your child. Tell or read stories that show how people show cooperation through their actions and deeds.

- Discuss ways that your family members cooperate with each other in your home.

- Set up "What Would You Do?" games. Use real or made-up situations to present your child with conflicts to work out. These games give children safe opportunities to practice making critical choices before they must make real-life choices.

- Help your child practice being cooperative in your own neighborhood.

These activities will empower your child to make positive choices and experience the impact and value of cooperation firsthand. Your assistance in reinforcing your child's education in good character is much appreciated.

Sincerely,

_____

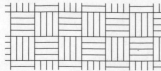

Standards Correlation

English Language Arts Standards	Page Numbers
1. Read a wide range of texts.	100, 101, 108, 109, 110, 115
2. Read a wide range of literature.	98, 102, 103, 112
3. Apply a variety of strategies to comprehend and interpret texts.	97, 98, 99, 100, 101, 102, 103, 106, 107, 108, 109, 110, 111, 112, 113, 115
4. Use spoken, written, and visual language to communicate effectively.	98, 99, 100, 101, 102, 103, 104, 106, 107, 108, 109, 110, 111, 113, 114
5. Use a variety of strategies while writing and use elements of the writing process to communicate.	98, 99, 100, 101, 104, 105, 106, 107, 108, 112, 113, 114, 115
6. Apply knowledge of language structure and conventions, media techniques, figurative language, and genre to create, critique, and discuss texts.	98, 99, 100, 101, 102, 103, 104, 106, 107, 112, 113, 114, 115
7. Research issues and interests, pose questions, and gather data to communicate discoveries.	97, 99, 104, 113, 114, 115
8. Work with a variety of technological and other resources to collect information and to communicate knowledge.	100, 101, 105, 108, 110, 111
9. Understand and respect the differences in language use across cultures, regions, and social roles.	98, 99, 100, 101, 102, 103, 104, 105, 112
10. Students whose first language is not English use their first language to develop competencies in English and other content areas.	98, 99, 100, 101, 102, 103, 104, 107, 108, 116
11. Participate in a variety of literary communities.	97, 98, 99, 100, 101, 103, 104, 105, 106, 107, 109, 110, 111, 112, 113, 114, 115
12. Use spoken, written, and visual language to accomplish purposes.	97, 98, 100, 101, 102, 104, 105, 106, 107, 108, 109, 110, 111, 112, 113, 114, 115

Social Studies Standards	
1. Culture: Compare similarities and differences between cultures. Describe the importance of cultural unity and diversity.	98, 100, 101, 102, 103, 115
2. Time, Continuity, and Change: Study people, places, and events of the past.	100, 101, 112, 116
3. People, Places, and Environments: Learn about geography and how people interact with the environment.	100, 101, 112, 116
4. Individual Development and Identity: Explore factors that contribute to one's personal identity.	97, 99, 104, 105, 108, 109, 110, 111, 113, 114
5. Individuals, Groups, and Institutions: Identify and describe the roles and influences of various institutions.	100, 101, 115, 116
6. Power, Authority, and Governance: Understand the purpose of government. Describe the rights and responsibilities of individuals and groups.	97, 98, 100, 101, 102, 103, 104, 105, 106, 107, 108, 113, 114, 115, 116
7. Production, Distribution, and Consumption: Explore how people organize to produce, distribute, and consume goods and services.	
8. Science, Technology, and Society: Describe ways in which science and technology have changed lives.	100, 101
9. Global Connections: Investigate how world societies depend on one another.	
10. Civic Ideals and Practices: Recognize the functions and ideals of a democratic government. Explain the rights and responsibilities of citizens.	97, 98, 100, 101, 102, 103, 104, 105, 106, 107, 108, 113, 114, 115, 116

Name _____

Are You a Cooperative Person?

Cooperation is defined as the act of working together to achieve a common goal. Cooperation happens when people act cooperatively in the following ways:

Cooperative people listen well to others.
Cooperative people share what they have with others.
Cooperative people take turns.
Cooperative people encourage other members of their team.
Cooperative people show appreciation for what others do to help them.
Cooperative people do their share of the work.
Cooperative people make sure that everyone in their group feels needed.
Cooperative people never leave anyone out.
Cooperative people compromise when they have a disagreement.

To find out how cooperative you are, use the scale to rate yourself for each of the actions shown by marking the number under the right column. Circle your choice for each action.

Cooperation Action	Almost Always	Sometimes	Not Very Often	Never
Listening well to others	3	2	1	0
Sharing what I have with others	3	2	1	0
Taking turns	3	2	1	0
Encouraging others	3	2	1	0
Showing appreciation for others' work	3	2	1	0
Doing my share of the job	3	2	1	0
Making everyone feel needed	3	2	1	0
Making sure that no one is left out	3	2	1	0
Compromising when I disagree with others	3	2	1	0
Totals:				

My total score: _____

How do you Rate? This rating scale can
be presented horizontally

    27–23: Master of Cooperation
    22–18: Master in Training
    17–13: Apprentice in Cooperation
     12–7: Beginner
  Below 7: Reform Candidate

Name _____

Quoting Cooperation

Cooperation is the act of working together to achieve a common goal. It requires that the members of the group or team act together as a team. Much has been said about the actions of a cooperative person. In this activity you will decide which action is being named for each of the quotes given. Use actions listed on page 97.

1. "It is easier to leave angry words unspoken than to mend a broken heart those words have broken." *Chinese Proverb*

   Action being described: _____

2. "Every pot must sit on its own bottom" *Benjamin Franklin*

   Action being described: _____

3. "If you have knowledge, let others light their candles at it." *Margaret Fuller*

   Action being described: _____

4. "Kind words can be short and easy to speak, but their echoes are truly endless" *Mother Teresa*

   Action being described: _____

5. "All of us do not have equal talent, but all of us should have an opportunity to develop our talents." *John F. Kennedy*

   Action being described: _____

6. "If we were supposed to talk more than we listen, we would have two mouths and one ear." *Mark Twain*

   Action being described: _____

7. "There are no free rides in society. We must pay to play." *Marva Collins*

   Action being described: _____

Name _____

Observing Cooperation

In this activity you will write down and keep a record of times and actions that you observe watching someone acting cooperatively. Remember that the actions of a cooperative person include listening to others, sharing what you have, taking turns, encouraging others, making sure that everyone feels needed, making sure that everyone is included, showing appreciation for what others do, and doing your best and part to help achieve your team's goal. You may observe members of your class, members of your family, people in a television show, people in a book you are reading, or people in a movie.

Example: Date: October 3rd: Observation: During lunch I saw Andrea invite the new girl Rochelle to sit at their table.

Action observed: Making sure that no one is left out.

Date: _____ Observation: _____
_____
Action observed: _____

Date: _____ Observation: _____
_____
Action observed:_____

Date: _____ Observation: _____
_____
Action observed: _____

Date: _____ Observation: _____
_____
Action Observed: _____

SUN   MON   TUES   WEDS   THURS   FRI   SAT

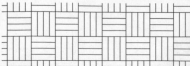

This is the story of a team of men and dogs who sought to achieve a common goal of being the first to reach The North Pole. The story began in 1881 on a hot steamy day in the Nicaraguan jungle as Lt. Robert E. Peary toiled to build a canal for the U.S. Corps of Civil Engineering. Peary sometimes thought about the cold Arctic regions of the North which he realized presented an opportunity for discovery and fame. He was not the first to set this goal as 756 other men had gone before him and given their lives while trying to achieve it.

Because his quest posed many dangers, it could not be achieved without the cooperation of many others. Peary's most valuable team member was Matthew Henson, an African American. Peary was so intrigued by Henson's stories of the sea that he hired him as a valet and asked him to return with him to Nicaragua. Henson was a man of many skills and soon impressed Peary so much that he was promoted to a survey assistant. Peary also asked Henson to join him in his quest to be the first man to reach the North Pole. Henson agreed.

Henson became an orphan at the age of eleven and was left under the care of an especially violent tempered stepmother. His first adventure began after a severe beating caused him to flee to Washington D.C., where he found work as a dishwasher. He listened to the tales of sailors about life at sea and he set out for Baltimore to pursue such a life. Henson's adventures at sea provided valuable navigational and people skills for the adventure with Peary to the North Pole.

To conquer the North Pole, Henson and Peary knew that they would need to learn as much as they could about the ways of life of the Eskimos. Henson learned the language and proved to be very skilled at dealing with and learning from the Eskimos. He worked as an interpreter and learned how to train dogs and sled teams. He learned how to build sledges and alcohol ovens, which could be used for both warmth and cooking. Adding to his talents were his strong navigational skills learned from his many years at sea. Peary had natural leadership abilities and the determination to succeed. Forged together, these talents allowed Henson and Peary to be successful where others had failed.

The realization of their goal began with a team of 23 men, 133 dogs, and 19 sleds. As the team traveled further and further north, their loads and number were reduced as sub-teams were sent ahead to perform the tasks of forging a trail, setting up camp, and building igloos. Supplies were brought to the camps from reserves kept at a land camp known as Crane City. As each sub-team completed their tasks, they were sent back to Crane City. The last of the sub-teams consisted of Henson, Peary, four Eskimos, and 40 dogs. It was these six men who would travel the remaining 133 miles to land a place in history. They planted the American flag into the North Pole on April 6, 1909 achieving a common goal set some 18 years before.

Name _____

Mapping Cooperation

1. What common goal did Henson and Peary have? _____

2. How did Henson help the team achieve its goal? _____

3. How did Peary help the team achieve its goal? _____

4. Do you think that either man could have achieved their common goal had they not worked
   together? _____ Why or why not? _____

To reach the North Pole, Matthew and Robert relied not only on cooperation, but also a map of the region. In this activity you will work with your team to map how you can show cooperation in different parts of your school.

Materials: map of your school, colored pencils, and this page

A. Find your classroom on your map. Then use one of your colored pencils to color it.

B. Make a key for your map and write the words "Our Classroom" in the key.

C. Draw a box beside the words "Our Classroom" and use the same color you chose to color it on the map to color in the box.

D. In the blank space on the back of your map write and complete the following:

   I can show cooperation in the (name the area) by _____.

E. Repeat steps A-D for each of the following places: the cafeteria, the gym, the playground, the hallway to our classroom, the auditorium, the music room, and the art room

5. In which area of your school does your group feel that it's most important to cooperate?

_____

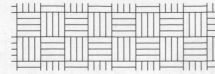

The One-Turnip Garden

This well-known Russian folk tale shows how working with others helps to achieve a goal.

Cast of Characters

Narrator	3rd Child
A Farmer	4th Child
Farmer's wife	1st Neighbor
1st Child	2nd Neighbor
2nd Child	

The Setting: A Russian farm

Narrator: It had been a particularly bad spring with very little rain and all of the vegetables in the farmer's garden had wilted and died except for one turnip plant that was still growing.

Farmer's wife: I'm worried. We have little food left in the house and everything in our garden has died except for our turnip plant.

Farmer: Don't worry. I'm sure our turnip plant will have a turnip tonight. I'll go check.

Narrator: So the farmer goes out to the garden where he sees that their turnip plant has produced a turnip that must weigh at least 50 pounds.

Farmer: This truly is a miracle plant for I've never seen a turnip this large. It will feed us for days when I pick it. (Farmer bends down to pick the turnip)

Narrator: The farmer pulls with all of his might, but the turnip won't budge from the earth. Just as he has fallen back, his wife comes out to the garden.

Farmer's wife: Oh my, that turnip could feed our family for a week. I'll bet I can pull it out.

Narrator: So the farmer's wife pulls with all of her strength, but still the turnip won't budge. As the farmer's wife is pulling, one of their children comes out to the garden.

1st Child: Oh my, that is the largest turnip I have ever seen. I'll bet I can pull it out.

Narrator: So the 1st child pulls until his muscles bulge, but still the turnip stays firmly planted. As the first child is pulling, a second child comes into the garden.

2nd Child: I can almost taste turnip soup. Here, let me try.

Narrator: So the second child pulls so hard that he falls backwards landing in the dry dirt of the garden. Just as the second child is falling backwards, the farmer's third child approaches and takes in the situation.

3rd Child: I have an idea. If we all pull together, I'll bet we can get our turnip out of the ground.

Farmer: What a good idea!

Narrator: So the farmer, his wife, and three of the children hold onto one another's waists and pull and pull but still the turnip won't come out. A neighbor walking by sees their distress and calls out.

Neighbor: Is everything okay?

Farmer: Our turnip plant has a turnip as large as a cow, but we pulled and pulled and we can't get it out of the ground.

1st Neighbor: (walking up to see) WOW! That is a large turnip. I'll bet if I pull, too, we can get that turnip to come out of the ground.

Narrator: So the farmer, his wife, three of their children, and their neighbor hold onto one another's waists to pull. Still they cannot wrestle the turnip from the ground.

1st Neighbor: (sighing) Maybe we should get more help.

Farmer to 1st child: Run to our neighbors and see if you can get us more help.

Narrator: So the farmer's oldest child runs to his neighbor's house and tells him about their problem. The neighbor agrees to help and together they return to the garden.

2nd Neighbor: That turnip could feed us all! Let me help.

Narrator: So the farmer, his wife, three of their children, and two of their neighbors hold onto one another's waists and pull, but still the turnip stays in the ground. Just as they are about to give up, the farmer's fourth child comes out to the garden.

4th Child: I am too small to help pull, but if you all try again, I will encourage the turnip to come out of the ground. Little turnip, you have grown big. You have grown gigantic! Now it is time to come up. (Having said this, the child takes their place at the end of the line.)

Narrator: So the farmer, his wife, four of their children, and two of their neighbors try again. This time the turnip comes out of the ground and the farmer, his wife, their children, and their neighbors enjoy a feast of fresh turnip soup, homemade bread, and a feeling of achievement for a job done well together.

Name _____

Write About It

Are You Listening?

One of the most important and difficult traits a cooperative person needs to show is the ability to listen well to others. In this activity you will act as a listener for one minute while your partner tells you a story about a time when he or she worked cooperatively with others to achieve a common goal. You will then summarize what you hear in the space provided. Your partner will then use the chart to rate how well you listened. You will then switch roles and your partner will become the listener.

Summary from Listener #1:

_____

_____

_____

_____

Rate Your Listener

Listening Action	Poor Job	Fair Job	Great Job
Leaned forward and faced the speaker			
Maintained eye contact			
Encouraged speaker by nodding and smiling			
Did not interrupt speaker			

Summary of Listener #2:

_____

_____

_____

_____

Rate Your Listener

Listening Action	Poor Job	Fair Job	Great Job
Leaned forward and faced the speaker			
Maintained eye contact			
Encouraged speaker by nodding and smiling			
Did not interrupt speaker			

Write About It

Cooperation In History

Throughout history, cooperation has played a role in shaping the outcome of many events. In this activity you will use reference books or the internet to complete each statement by identifying the goal accomplished by each team.

1. Lewis and Clark worked together with Sacagawea to_____
   _____

2. Rachel Brown and Elizabeth Hazen worked together to _____
   _____

3. Harriett Tubman and the Underground Railroad worked together to
   _____

4. Bernard Silver and Norman Joseph Woodland worked together to
   _____

5. The crew of Apollo 11, Buzz Aldrin, Neil Armstrong, and Michael Collins worked together to
   _____
   _____

6. Emile and his son Henry Berliner worked together to_____
   _____

7. Paul Revere, William Dawes, and Samuel Prescott worked together to _____
   _____

8. Alfred Vail and Samuel Morse worked together to_____
   _____

0-7682-2795-X *Character Education*

Cooperation in Action

In this activity you will work in small groups to role-play how the different actions of a cooperative person can be shown in each of the situations described.

Action: Listening well to others

Hernando is a good listener. People are always going to him because he almost always looks the person speaking in the eye, focuses on what they are saying, doesn't interrupt them while they are speaking, and repeats what they have said when they have finished to make sure that he understands them. Role play how Hernando acts when he is listening to others.

Action: Sharing what you have with others

Francine almost always has a smile ready to share with someone else. She helps others in the library by sharing the name of a good book she has read and is never hesitant to share her ideas with her group. Francine also shares her time with others and is never too busy for a friend. Role play how Francine acts to make sure that she shares what she has with others.

Action: Taking turns with others

Jason almost always makes sure that he is not always the first or last person in line. He uses his time sparingly on the school computer so that others can have a chance to use it. He also waits patiently to get a drink of water at the water fountain and then counts to 10 to make sure that the next person doesn't have to wait too long. Role play how Jason acts to make sure that he takes turns with others.

Action: Showing appreciation for others work

Mrs. Lester almost always lets students in her class know how much she appreciates what they do. She is quick with a "Thank you" for students who help out in the classroom. She lets students know how much she appreciates their hard work by using stickers and writing positive comments on their papers. Role play how Mrs. Lester acts to show appreciation for her students' work.

Action: Encouraging others

Mr. Renaldi almost always encourages students in his band class. He is quick to point out that Louis Armstrong did not learn to play the trumpet in a day. He also notices when a student is down and offers his time to listen. Mr. Renaldi lets students come in at lunch and after school for extra practice. He never puts a student down and is always has a positive word of encouragement. Role play how Mr. Renaldi acts to encourage the students in his band class.

Action: Making sure that everyone feels needed

Mr. Brockman almost always makes sure that everyone in his art class feels needed. He asks students to be in charge of different jobs like cleaning the paint brushes, passing out the supplies, and cleaning the tables. He makes sure that everyone in the class has a job to do that helps the class succeed. Mr. Brockman changes jobs each week so that everyone has a chance to do different jobs. Role play how Mr. Brockman acts to make sure that the students in his class feel needed.

Action: Compromising when you have a disagreement

Felicity almost always gives in a little whenever she disagrees with someone else. She makes sure that she tries to see their side by listening to what they have to say. She offers suggestions as to how their disagreement can be worked out and almost never uses an angry voice. If she cannot reach a compromise she seeks the help of her teacher to try and resolve the problem. Role-play how Felicity might act whenever she has a disagreement with someone.

Questions to Consider:

1. How do the different actions that you role-played work together to achieve cooperation?

_____

2. Which action does your team think is the most important one to show when you are working with others?

_____

Name _____

Cooperation at Home

During this unit we have focused mostly on cooperation at school, but it is also important to show cooperation at home and in your community. Talk with your family to come up with a plan that shows how cooperation is important in each of the situations.

Situation 1:
Your family only has one television that gets cable and everyone wants to watch a different program at the same time.

_____

_____

_____

Situation 2:
Everyone in your family has to get ready for work or school in the morning.

_____

_____

_____

Situation 3:
Your family only has one car to use and three of your family members have to be somewhere at about the same time.

_____

_____

_____

Discuss other ways in which your family shows cooperation with other family members.

Name _____

Paper Toll Bridges

Through cooperation we are able to accomplish more. In this activity you will be working together to see how strong four sheets of paper can be as they work together to make a bridge that is able to support a cup of pennies.

Materials: 4 sheets of plain white paper, 6 small paperclips, scissors, a ruler, 2 empty 5-oz paper cups, and 50 pennies.

1. Use the ruler to measure a distance of 30 centimeters and then place an empty cup at each end of your measurement.

2. Use the plain white paper and 6 paperclips to build a bridge that is able to cross the space between the cups. The bridge may not be attached to the cups.

3. Give some of the pennies to each team member.

4. Test your bridge's strength by having team members take turns carefully placing a penny on top of the bridge. Then another student follows the same procedure. Continue to take turns placing pennies on your bridge until your bridge falls or sags to meet the surface you are working on.

5. Count the number of pennies your bridge held and write this number down in the space provided.

6. Use the table to rate how well your group worked together.

Our bridge held _____ pennies before it collapsed.

How does your group rate?

Cooperative Action	1–poorly	2–okay	3–great
Listening to each other			
Sharing ideas and information			
Encouraging others and showing appreciation			
Making sure that everyone feels needed			
Compromising when there were conflicts			

Total Rating: _____

Cooperation Tree

We use a dictionary to find the meaning of a word. There are other words known as synonyms that have the same meaning and can be used in place of a word. Words that have the opposite meaning are known as antonyms. Both synonyms and antonyms can be found in a special resource tool called a thesaurus. In this activity you will be using both a dictionary and a thesaurus to find and classify words that are like cooperation and words that are the opposite of cooperation. Answer the questions on page 111.

Materials: a large sheet of colored paper, lined index cards, a thesaurus, a dictionary, colored pencils or markers, glue, and a cooperative group

1. Use one of your colored pencils or markers to write the word cooperation at the top of one of your index cards.

2. Find the word cooperation in your dictionary and then write its definition on the card you made in step 1.

3. Use a different colored pencil or marker to write the word synonym at the top of another index card.

4. Find the word synonym in your dictionary and then write its definition on the card you made in step 2.

5. Use your thesaurus to find at least two synonyms for the word cooperation.

6. Write the words you found in step 5 on separate cards using the same color you used for your synonym card.

7. Find both words in the dictionary and then write the definition for each synonym on its card.

8. Use a different colored pencil or marker to write the word Antonym at the top of another index card and repeat steps 4–7 for antonyms your group found.

9. Glue your cards to make a tree diagram as shown below:

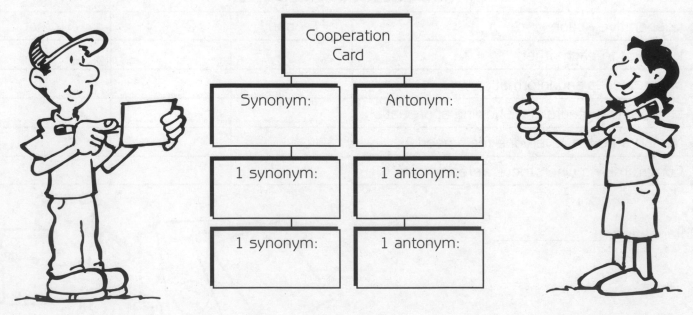

Questions to Consider

1. Which group of words has the same meaning? _____

   Which group has the opposite meaning? _____

2. Why does your group think we used different colors for each group of words?

   _____

3. What tools did your group use for this assignment?

   _____ and _____

4. Compare: How are these research tools alike?

   _____

5. Contrast: How are these tools different?

   _____

6. Why do you think it is important to include antonyms in an assignment on cooperation?

   _____

Name _____

Lesson in Fire

Once there was a very wise farmer whose seven sons argued and bickered constantly so that they could never work together to accomplish any of the many chores that running a farm required. The wise farmer knew that if his sons could find a way to work together, their chores would be easier and their spirits would be better. He tried to provide as many opportunities as he could to encourage his sons to work together. However, each time the sons were together, they spent their time arguing about who should do what or how the work should be done and the work remained undone.

After much time the farmer came up with a plan to show his sons how to achieve a goal by working together. He called his sons to the field one cold and windy evening and gave them each a single stick of firewood to build a fire to warm themselves. He watched as each of his sons tried in vain to get their fire going. After many matches had been spent and still the sons had no fire to warm the chilly evening air, the wise father asked that each son bring their stick of firewood to him. As they watched, he laid one stick upon another to form a pile.

Beneath this pile he placed shaved pieces of his own stick to serve as kindling. He then struck a single match and ignited the kindling, which in turn ignited each stick of firewood until a roaring fire leapt up and chased away the chill of the evening air. The wise father then told his sons that they were like the single sticks of firewood. Working alone, they could do very little; but by working together with each one contributing something, they could do great things.

He also told them that the sticks of wood could not have worked together without the encouragement of the kindling. Like the single stick used to start the fire, each of them must give of themselves by sharing what they have, encouraging their fellow brothers, and compromising in time of conflict. So it was that the brothers were warmed not only by the heat of the fire, but also by the spirit of cooperation which continued to warm them far beyond the chilly night.

What is the moral of this fable?

_____

_____

_____

_____

_____

_____

_____

_____

0-7682-2795-X *Character Education*

Name _____

Cooperative Looking Glass

Throughout this unit you have been asked to observe cooperation, work cooperatively with others, identify and role-play the actions of cooperative people. Take this time to reflect on what you have learned about cooperation.

1. The most important thing I have learned about cooperation is _____

   because _____

   _____

2. My cooperative action score was _____ which means _____

   _____

   _____

3. The cooperative action I am best at is_____

   _____

4. The cooperative action that I need the most improvement on is_____

   _____

   I can improve this action by _____

   _____

5. I need to show cooperation at school because _____

   _____

It is important for me to cooperate at home because _____

_____

_____

_____

_____

Name _____

My Personal Cooperation Log

Cooperation Trait	Example of a time I showed this trait
Listening well to others	
Sharing what I have with others	
Taking turns	
Encouraging other members of my group or team	
Showing appreciation for the work others do	
Making sure everyone felt needed	
Doing my share of the work	
Making sure that no one was left out	
Giving in a little when I had a disagreement with a teammate	

Extension Activities

Graphing Cooperation Posters:

Objective: To provide students with an opportunity to collect and interpret data through a survey and graph.

Materials: Data table, graph paper, student results from quiz on page 97, colored pencils, scissors, poster board, and glue

1. Hand out the data table shown below and have students fill it in as the class is surveyed. An overhead would work well.

Cooperation Trait	# of Almost Always	# of Sometimes	# of Not very often	# of Never
Listens to others				
Shares				
Takes Turns				
Compromise				
Does their part				
Shows Appreciation				
Encourages				
Makes people feel needed				
Doesn't exclude				

2. Divide students into teams of two or three students each and give each team a trait.

3. Instruct students to create a bar graph that shows the results of the class survey for their trait. Remind them to include labels and a title.

4. Direct students to put their completed graph on a poster board that also includes the following information: Definition of cooperation, summary statement of what the graph shows, and pictures of their traits.

5. Have students share their posters with the rest of the class.

Discussion Questions: Which trait ranks highest for your class? Which trait shows a need for most improvement?

Cooperative Want Ad

Objective: To provide pairs of students with an opportunity to write a want ad that identifies the actions a cooperative person shows

Materials: page 97 and a large index card:

1. Pass out a copy of page 97 to each student and have them rate themselves on their cooperation skills.

2. Next, have students work in pairs. Direct them to write a want ad for a cooperative person. Have them create a job description that includes the actions a cooperative person needs to show. Rank them in the order of importance.

Questions for Discussion: Poll the class to determine which actions they considered most important by having each pair of students identify the action they chose and the reason for their choice. Ask students to identify which cooperative actions they practiced while doing this activity.

Spelling Relays

Objective: To provide students with an opportunity to practice the traits of a cooperative person as they work together to achieve a common goal.

Materials: student teams, list of spelling words, and a chalkboard

1. Go over the rules of the relay as shown below:

   A. The first player goes to the board and writes only the first letter of the word.

   B. The first player then returns to the team and the second player goes to the board to write the next letter of the word.

   C. Each player can only write one letter.

   D. Players in line may not call out answers to player at board.

   E. Players may encourage and show appreciation when player returns to line.

   F. The first team to spell the word correctly gets 2 points.

2. Divide the class into teams and proceed with the relay.

Discussion Question: Which traits of a cooperative person did we practice?

Adopt a Park

Objective: To provide students with an opportunity to work cooperatively within their community.

1. Use a map to have students find a park that is within walking distance of the school. If one cannot be found, adopt the playground.

2. Have students visit the park or playground to create a list of jobs to be done.

3. Upon their return, compile the jobs to create a class list.

4. Have students sign up for the different jobs they selected.

5. Return to the park or playground so that students can complete their tasks.

6. Change jobs and arrange other visits as your schedule permits.

Respect

Note for Teachers:

This unit is designed to help fifth graders learn about respect and to encourage them to develop good character. The activities in this unit, which are tied to national language arts and social studies standards, help students explore several aspects of respectful behavior through interactive writing, reading, and cooperative projects. Students realize that respect is the foundation that allows them to develop other positive character traits such as tolerance, responsibility, and cooperation. Best of all, students will be introduced to the positive impact and value of being a respectful person, while learning the importance of making positive choices for themselves.

Dear Parent or Guardian:

Our class is participating in a character-building unit of study on respect. Together we will explore the many aspects of respect and participate in activities that aim to strengthen each student's understanding of respect within our community.

You are invited to share in your child's learning experience by continuing the process of teaching him or her about respect at home. You can do this in several ways:

- Be aware of the way you model respect. Ask your child questions about respect or share your views of respect with your child.

- Select a historical person whom you think has a strong sense of respect. Talk about this person with your child. Tell or read stories that show how respectful people act.

- Discuss the ways your family expresses respect for each other in your home. Talk about your values for respecting all living things as well as respecting property and the environment.

- Set up "What Would You Do?" games. Use real or made-up situations to present your child with conflicts to work out. These games give children safe opportunities to practice making critical choices before they must make real choices that may have serious consequences.

- Help your child find ways to practice respect in the neighborhood.

These activities will empower your child to make positive choices and experience the impact and value of respect firsthand. Your cooperation and assistance in reinforcing your child's education in good character is much appreciated.

Sincerely,

_____

Standards Correlation

English Language Arts Standards	Page Numbers
1. Read a wide range of texts.	122, 124, 125, 128, 129, 134
2. Read a wide range of literature.	122, 124, 125, 134
3. Apply a variety of strategies to comprehend and interpret texts.	123, 125, 128, 129, 134
4. Use spoken, written, and visual language to communicate effectively.	120, 121, 123, 125, 127, 128, 129, 130, 131, 132, 133, 134, 135, 136
5. Use a variety of strategies while writing and use elements of the writing process to communicate.	134
6. Apply knowledge of language structure and conventions, media techniques, figurative language, and genre to create, critique, and discuss texts.	125, 128, 129, 132, 133, 134
7. Research issues and interests, pose questions, and gather data to communicate discoveries.	121, 130, 131, 135, 136
8. Work with a variety of technological and other resources to collect information and to communicate knowledge.	
9. Understand and respect the differences in language use across cultures, regions, and social roles.	128, 129, 131, 133
10. Students whose first language is not English use their first language to develop competencies in English and other content areas.	
11. Participate in a variety of literary communities.	
12. Use spoken, written, and visual language to accomplish purposes.	119, 120, 121, 123, 125, 126, 127, 128, 129, 130, 131, 132, 133, 134, 135, 136

Social Studies Standards	
1. Culture: Compare similarities and differences between cultures. Describe the importance of cultural unity and diversity.	
2. Time, Continuity, and Change: Study people, places, and events of the past.	
3. People, Places, and Environments: Learn about geography and how people interact with the environment.	122, 123, 124, 125
4. Individual Development and Identity: Explore factors that contribute to one's personal identity.	
5. Individuals, Groups, and Institutions: Identify and describe the roles and influences of various institutions.	119, 120, 123, 125, 126, 127, 128, 129, 130, 131, 132, 133, 134, 135, 136
6. Power, Authority, and Governance: Understand the purpose of government. Describe the rights and responsibilities of individuals and groups.	
7. Production, Distribution, and Consumption: Explore how people organize to produce, distribute, and consume goods and services.	
8. Science, Technology, and Society: Describe ways in which science and technology have changed lives.	
9. Global Connections: Investigate how world societies depend on one another.	
10. Civic Ideals and Practices: Recognize the functions and ideals of a democratic government. Explain the rights and responsibilities of citizens.	

Name _____

What Does Respect Mean?

If you have ever made a pizza, you know that you start with the crust. You roll out the dough and place it on the pizza pan. You pat the dough firmly in place and make sure that there are no holes in it. Then you add the sauce, the cheese, and the toppings.

1. Why is the crust an important part of the pizza?

_____

_____

_____

Respect is a character trait that is similar to the crust of a pizza. Just as the crust gives a pizza a solid base, respect for yourself and others gives you the solid base you need to develop other good character traits. Respect is the foundation that allows you to become more tolerant, cooperative, and responsible.

Respect means being courteous and polite to others. A respectful person listens to others and uses kind words. Respect means treating others the way you would like others to treat you.

2. How could being courteous and polite help you become a more tolerant person?

_____

_____

Respect also means showing consideration to others. People who are considerate accept and honor other people's feelings, ideas, beliefs, and differences.

3. How could being considerate help you become a more cooperative person?

_____

_____

Respect involves caring for yourself, your family, school, community, the environment, the earth, and all the creatures on it.

4. How could caring for yourself, others, and the earth help you become a more responsible person?

_____

_____

Name _____

Self-Respect and Respect for Others

If you have self-respect, you think of yourself as a valuable, worthy person. You take care of yourself mentally, emotionally, and physically. You don't put yourself down in your own mind or out loud to your friends. You show respect to someone very important—you!

1. Place a checkmark next to each action that shows self-respect.

   _____ When Loren is discouraged about his math grade, he reminds himself that he is working hard and will improve.

   _____ Rhonda says, "I'm not very good" when her friends compliment her singing.

   _____ Jamahl walks the dog everyday to get exercise.

   _____ Maria smokes marijuana with her older brother.

   _____ Josh talks to a counselor when he is concerned about something.

2. List two other actions that show self-respect.

   _____

   _____

3. Treating others with respect will be easier if you respect yourself. Place a checkmark next to each action that shows respect for others.

   _____ Trent greets his math teacher by saying "Good morning, Mr. Andrews."

   _____ Corey answers the phone by saying "What do you want?"

   _____ Alexia puts down Gina because she doesn't like Gina's clothes.

   _____ Juan takes time to listen to Victor's ideas.

   _____ Marisol doesn't make fun of Ryan's lisp.

4. List two other actions that show respect for others.

   _____

   _____

   _____

   _____

Name _____

Get permission to watch two shows on television during the week. In the first box below, record each example you see of respectful behavior by any of the characters. In the second box below, record examples where you think behavior could be improved.

Respectful Behavior

_____
_____
_____
_____
_____
_____
_____
_____

Disrespectful Behavior

_____
_____
_____
_____
_____
_____
_____
_____

1. Were there more examples of respectful or of disrespectful behavior in the shows you watched?

_____
_____

2. How did other characters respond to someone who acted respectfully? To someone who acted disrespectfully?

_____
_____

3. What conclusions can you draw about what you saw on television?

_____
_____

Share your thoughts with your classmates.

Albert Schweitzer was born in 1875 in Germany. He studied music, theology, and philosophy at Strasbourg University. Even as a young man, Albert knew he wanted to serve people who were suffering. When he was twenty-four, he decided to practice medicine in an area of central Africa which was then called the Congo. To get ready, Albert studied medicine for eight years. In 1913, he and his wife Helene sailed to Africa. They started a hospital in an old chicken coop in Lambarene. He was the only doctor in the area. People came from miles around suffering from malaria, ulcers, hernias, leprosy, and the sleeping sickness caused by tsetse flies.

While the Schweitzers were in Africa, two world wars occurred in Europe. The French controlled the Congo at that time. Since the Schweitzers were German citizens by birth, they were considered enemies by the French. They were placed under house arrest in Lambarene and not allowed to practice medicine.

During this period, Albert had time to think deeply about many issues. He wondered why people murdered others and destroyed things. He tried to find a key to understanding life. One day when he was traveling on the Ogowe River, he saw four hippopotami caring for their young. He realized then that so many people mistreated each other because they did not care for each other. He believed that only by caring for and respecting each other, could people treat others and all living creatures better. He called his idea "reverence for life." He believed it was the key to opening minds and hearts, and to curing humanity.

Many people throughout the world became interested in his work and in his ideas about reverence for life. In 1952, Albert Schweitzer won the Nobel Peace Prize. He used the money to build a village for his leprosy patients. He died in 1965 at the age of 90.

Name _____

Respect in Action: Albert Schweitzer

1. Why did Albert Schweitzer decide to practice medicine in the Congo?

_____

_____

2. What kinds of things did Albert Schweitzer think about while he was under house arrest?

_____

_____

3. What did Dr. Schweitzer see while he was traveling on the Ogowe River?

_____

_____

4. What did Dr. Schweitzer realize from this experience?

_____

_____

_____

5. Dr. Schweitzer believed that only if people cared for and respected each other, could they treat others and all living creatures better. What did he call this idea?

_____

_____

6. Who do you know that treats every living thing with respect?

_____

_____

7. What does this person do to show respect?

_____

President Jimmy Carter

Read this short play silently or aloud together with your class.

Characters: *Teacher, Shelby, Nathan, Courtney, Jacob*

Setting: *Students are discussing American presidents in their social studies class.*

Teacher: We have had many fine presidents since this country began in 1776. Some of the presidents really stand out because they have been men of good character. For example, if I mention the trait of honesty, which president do you think of?

Shelby: Well, we've all heard of Abraham Lincoln's honesty. When he worked in a store as a young boy, he walked several miles to return a few cents to a woman he had accidentally overcharged.

Teacher: That's an excellent example. Now, if we talk about the trait of respect, which president comes to mind?

Courtney: How about former President Jimmy Carter? When he left office, President Carter started to build houses for people who needed them. He's still doing that, I think.

Teacher: You're right, Courtney. President Carter works with a group called "Habitat for Humanity." Groups of volunteers work together to build houses for people who could not otherwise afford them.

Teacher: Does anyone know another way that President Carter shows respect for others?

Nathan: I think he resolves a lot of conflicts between nations.

Jacob: Didn't he help resolve a conflict in the Middle East when he was president?

Teacher: Yes, he helped bring about peace between Egypt and Israel. He learned to resolve conflicts as a young boy living in the segregated South. Do you remember what "segregation" means?

Shelby: Segregation meant that black people were not allowed to go to school or ride a bus or join many other activities with white people.

Teacher: Yes, that's correct. Jimmy Carter's parents taught their son to have a deep respect for people's differences. They also taught him that almost all human conflicts can be solved peacefully.

Courtney: He still travels around the world to resolve conflicts, doesn't he?

Teacher: He has helped settle disputes in many countries. His goal is to ensure peace and human rights for all people. He works with the Carter Center in Georgia to unite people and resources to resolve conflicts. The Center tries to find ways to help erase hunger, disease, and violations of human rights around the world.

Nathan: I'm really impressed.

Teacher: I think we all agree that President Carter stands out as an excellent example of respect in action.

Think and Discuss:

After reading the play, think about the following questions and discuss them with your classmates.

How does building a house for someone who cannot afford it show respect?

How does solving a conflict between two groups of people show respect?

How does erasing hunger and disease show respect for others?

Jimmy Carter has said:

To work for better understanding among people, one does not have to be a former president sitting at a fancy conference room table. Peace can be made in the neighborhoods, the living rooms, the playing fields, and the classrooms of our country.

Name _____

Writing About Self-Respect

Self-respect is the cornerstone for respecting others. Self-respect is what lets you act in positive ways. It is easier to respect others if you respect yourself.

Grace receives a high grade on an essay that she wrote for social studies class. She worked very hard on the essay, but when a friend congratulated her, she put herself down by saying, "Oh, I guess it was just my lucky day."

Think about the words or phrases you sometimes use to put yourself down. Make a list of the words and phrases below.

_____

_____

Go back to your list above and draw an X through each of the negative words and phrases. Try not to use those words and phrases again!

Next to each phrase on the left below, write words of encouragement. An example is done for you.

1. "I'll never be able to do that."_____ "I'll give it a try." _____

2. "I might as just as well give up." _____

3. "I'm too dumb to learn math." _____

Imagine that Justin just won an award for perfect attendance at school. If Justin does not have self-respect, he might respond to a compliment by saying, "It was nothing." If Justin has self-respect, he might say, "Thanks, I made an effort to get to school everyday."

Now read the example below.

Janna organized a school-wide clean up day. She assigned each grade an area of the school grounds to clean. Her teacher congratulated her for her fine work. How should Janna respond?

_____

_____

Name _____

Respecting Your Ideas and Those of Others

1. Why do you think some people tease and put down others who do not always follow the path of the "in" thing to do?

   _____

   _____

   _____

   _____

2. What is your reaction when someone puts you down, teases you, or gossips about you?

   _____

   _____

   _____

3. Do you think people who put down others have self-respect? Explain your ideas.

   _____

   _____

   _____

4. How can teasing and cruel gossip sometimes lead to physical violence? Explain..

   _____

   _____

   _____

5. How do YOU respect the difference in other people?

   _____

   _____

   _____

   _____

   _____

   _____

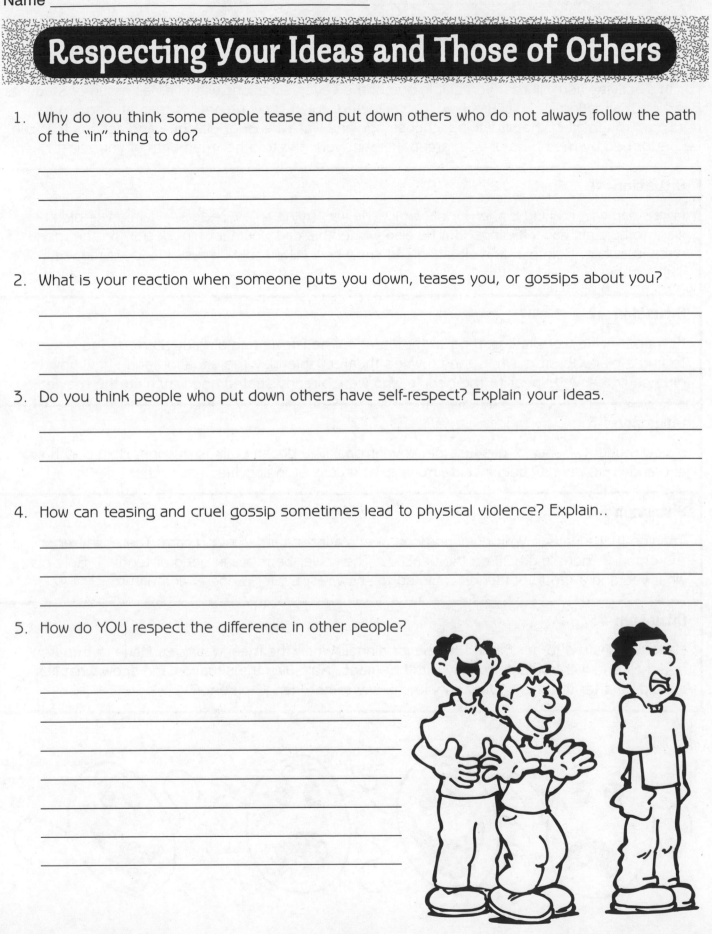

0-7682-2795-X *Character Education*

Playing Your Part

For this activity, you will cast yourself in one of the seven situations with a small group of students. Read each situation and discuss how the characters could show respect in that situation. After reading through all of the situations, choose one and write ideas for dialogue and actions that can be performed by members of your group. Present your skit to other members of your class.

Situation #1

Mike's dad was making dinner for his family. He was trying a new recipe—again. Mike didn't want to hurt his dad's feelings, but he also wished his dad would let him decide on the menu once in awhile. Role-play the situation and show how Mike could discuss his ideas respectfully with his dad.

Situation #2

Kim and Vickie were late getting to the theater. The movie had already started. They needed to find a place to sit down in the crowded theater. Role-play the situation and show how the girls could show respect to the people who were already seated and watching the movie.

Situation #3

A new student, Roberto, has just joined your class. He doesn't talk to anyone. Role-play how you and your friends could include Roberto at recess or in activities after school.

Situation #4

Imagine that a park in your neighborhood needs a lot of tender loving care. There is litter on the ground. There is graffiti on the benches. The flower beds are in need of tending. Role-play what you and a group of friends could do to show respect for property and nature.

Situation #5

Marie was invited to her friend's house for dinner. When the meal was over, Marie got up from her chair and went outside to play with her friend. Role-play the situation and show what Marie should do after the meal. What should she say to her friend's parents?

Playing Your Part

Situation #6

Kyle had been playing football and he was hungry. At supper, Kyle dumped all the potatoes on his plate. Kyle then grabbed three pork chops and the last piece of bread. Role-play the situation. Show what Kyle should do and what he should say to the other members of his family.

Situation #7

All the students were in line waiting for tickets to the movie. Francine did not want to wait at the end of the line. She saw some friends at the front of the line. They told her to join them at the front of the line. Role-play this scene. What should Francine do and say in this situation?

Discuss with your group your choice of the above scenarios. Then create dialogue and decide on your presentation to other members of your class. Be certain to have your skit demonstrate the characteristic of respect.

Name _____

School-to-Home Connection

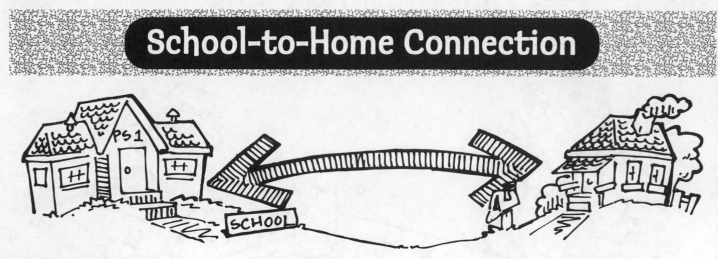

Take this paper home and use it to interview a member of your family. You can interview a parent or guardian, a grandparent, or other adult relative. Record the person's answers on the lines beneath each question. Bring the results of your interview back to school so you can share it with your class.

1. Please tell me about an event in your life in which you, or another person you know, demonstrated great respect.

   _____

   _____

   _____

2. Describe the action that demonstrated respect.

   _____

   _____

   _____

3. What kinds of words did you or the other person use to show respect?

   _____

   _____

   _____

4. How did others respond to the way you or the other person showed respect?

   _____

   _____

   _____

5. How did self-respect affect what you or the other person did?

   _____

   _____

Getting It Together

For this activity, you will work in small groups. Read and follow the instructions below.

1. Each group should have several pairs of scissors, a glue stick, four large pieces of construction paper, and a copy of this instruction sheet. Each member of the group should have a copy of the Record Sheet and a copy of the Summary Sheet on pages 132 and 133.

2. Each group should write one of the following titles on each piece of construction paper: Self-Respect, Respect for Others, Respect for Property, Respect for the World.

3. Each member of the group should complete the sentences on the Record Sheet.

4. Each member of the group should cut out the four boxes on the Record Sheet.

5. Group members then place their sentences in a collection box on the teacher's desk.

6. The teacher will mix up the sentences from all the groups.

7. A member of each group will pull out sentences randomly from the box. Divide the sentences equally among all groups.

8. Members of the groups take turns reading a sentence aloud to the rest of the group. The members decide on which piece of construction paper to glue the sentence.

9. After all the sentences have been glued to the pieces of construction paper, the group chooses their favorite example from each category (Self-Respect, Respect for Others, Respect for Property, Respect for the World). The group writes that example on the appropriate place on the Summary Sheet. Based on their examples, each group formulates a definition of respect.

10. Groups share their Summary Sheets with the rest of the class.

Name ________________________________

Record Sheet

We show respect for ourselves when . . .

____

____

____

We show respect for ourselves when . . .

____

____

____

We show respect for ourselves when . . .

____

____

____

We show respect for ourselves when . . .

____

____

____

Summary Sheet

Members of our Group: _____

_____

_____

Our favorite examples: _____

We show respect for ourselves when . . .

_____

_____

We show respect for others when . . .

_____

_____

We show respect for property when . . .

_____

_____

We show respect for the world when . . .

_____

_____

Our group's definition of respect:

_____

_____

_____

_____

0-7682-2795-X *Character Education*

Name _____

Do you remember the fable about the lion and the mouse?

In that fable, a tiny mouse is about to be eaten by a lion. The mouse begs the lion not to eat him. He tells the lion that perhaps someday he will be able to help him. The lion laughs at the idea of a tiny mouse helping a mighty lion. Nonetheless, the lion lets the mouse go. Some time later, the lion is caught in a hunter's net and cannot escape. His roars of pain alert the little mouse, who comes to the lion's rescue by gnawing through the ropes and freeing the lion.

In that fable, the lion and the mouse show respect for each other. The lesson in the story is that a "kindness is never wasted."

Another fable tells about an ant and a dove. In this fable, an ant falls into a brook. The ant cannot reach the shore and is about to drown. A dove who is nearby drops a blade of straw into the water. The ant climbs onto the straws and floats to shore. A little while later, the ant sees a man getting ready to kill the dove with a stone. Just as the man threw the stone, the ant stung him in the heel. That made the man miss his aim, and the startled dove flew to safety.

1. How is this story like the lion and the mouse?

   _____

   _____

   _____

   _____

2. What is the lesson in these stories?

   _____

   _____

   _____

   _____

On the back of this page, create your own fable about respect.

Name _____

Reflecting on Respect

One good thing leads to another! As you become more respectful, you are also becoming more responsible, cooperative, and tolerant. Think about three respectful things that you have done or said during the past week that show you are also becoming more responsible, cooperative, or tolerant. List each item in the appropriate box below.

Responsible
_____
_____
_____

Cooperative
_____
_____
_____

Tolerant
_____
_____
_____

Rate Yourself! Circle the number below that shows how respectful you are.

1	2	3	4	5	6	7	8	9	10
Need Work on Respect				Somewhat Respectful				Very Respectful	

One thing I could do or say to show respect:

_____
_____

135   0-7682-2795-X *Character Education*

Name _____

© McGraw-Hill Children's Publishing

Keeping a Journal

Keep this journal for two weeks. Write down all the ways you showed respect in each area below. Use this along with self-reflection assignment on page 135.

Self-Respect	Respect for my family

Respect for my neighborhood	Respect for other students

Respect for my teachers	Respect for animals

Respect for property	Respect for my country

Respect for law	Respect for the environment

Encourage students to extend their learning about respect with these engaging activities.

Observe and Discuss

Ask students to observe the level of respect they see at school between students, or between students and teachers. Discuss their observations as a class. What did they observe people doing or saying to show respect to others? Also discuss the effect each act of respect had on another person. Add your own observations to the discussion.

Create a Respect Bulletin Board

Photograph students and teachers you see demonstrating respect throughout your school. Enlarge the pictures on the copying machine. Then show the pictures to your students and ask them to identify what the person is doing in each picture. Put the pictures on the bulletin board.

Write about Respect

Ask students to write a poem about things they do that show how much they respect themselves. Display the poems on a classroom bulletin board or other prominent area.

Celebrate Diversity

Set aside a day to celebrate the diversity of cultures that are represented in your school and community. Ask students to share one aspect of their cultural heritage such as a song, costume, game, custom, or recipe.

Extension Activities

Listen to Songs

Play songs for students about respect including Aretha Franklin's "R-E-S-P-E-C-T." Provide copies of the lyrics for students. Ask students to consider why people might write songs about respect. As a follow-up, ask students to write their own songs about respect. Some students may want to perform their songs for the class.

Field Trip

Organize a field trip or project focused on the idea of respect for the world. This could be a beach cleanup, creation of a flower or vegetable garden, establishment of a bird feeding area, or the maintenance of such areas. Ask students to brainstorm ideas for such a trip or project.

Talk about the News

Tell students about current events in which a person showed respect. Mention the names of citizens, civic leaders, and school officials who show respect.

Go on a Scavenger Hunt

Send students on a scavenger hunt through magazines. They may choose either "respect" or "disrespect" as their topic. Have them make a collage of examples of their topics and explain to the class how each picture communicates respect or disrespect.

Keep a Character Log

Create a classroom character log in which students can record the names and deeds of characters they read about who demonstrate respect. Students should also record the title and author of the book. From time to time, ask students to discuss the books and characters with the class.

Tolerance

Dear Teacher:

The activities in this unit are designed to help teach tolerance. Tolerance is having a fair and objective attitude towards those whose opinions, practices, race, religion, or nationality may be different from our own. A tolerant person is someone who respects other people, regardless of how they differ from themselves. Helping students to focus on how we are all alike instead of how we differ allows us to become more tolerant towards one another.

The first teacher extension, Declaration of Tolerance, is an excellent springboard to use in launching the unit. Student activity pages include writing activities, a reader's theater, role-playing activities, and hands-on activities. Students learn to identify and internalize the traits and behaviors associated with tolerance.

Materials needed and teacher set-up time is minimal to allow you more time to teach. All activities and extensions provided in this book are directly related to the National Language Arts and Social Studies Standards as identified on the next page.

Dear Parent or Guardian:

Our class is working to build good character. In this unit, we are working on tolerance. A tolerant person is someone who respects other people, regardless of how they differ from themselves. We have outlined some steps that can help us become more tolerant of others. These include:

- standing up for others who are being bullied for being different
- taking time to get to know someone before forming an opinion
- seeing others for how they are alike instead of how they are different
- learning about the cultures and practices of others
- appreciating and enjoying people who are different
- treating everyone in the manner in which we want to be treated

Since tolerance is needed both at home and in the classroom, we ask that you discuss with your child ways they can show more tolerance towards others. Commend your child when you "catch them" being tolerant of someone else. During this unit we will also be sending home an activity to be completed with your family.

Working together, we can achieve the goal of helping your child become a more tolerant person. Thank you for your support and the positive role model that you provide to your child.

Sincerely,

_____

English Language Arts Standards	Page Numbers
1. Read a wide range of texts.	142, 144, 145, 146, 147, 148, 149, 150, 151, 153, 154, 155, 157, 158, 159
2. Read a wide range of literature.	156, 160
3. Apply a variety of strategies to comprehend and interpret texts.	142, 143, 144, 145, 146, 147, 148, 149, 150, 151, 153, 154, 155, 156, 157, 158, 160
4. Use spoken, written, and visual language to communicate effectively.	141, 142, 143, 144, 145, 146, 147, 148, 149, 150, 151, 152, 153, 154, 155, 156, 157, 158, 159, 160
5. Use a variety of strategies while writing and use elements of the writing process to communicate.	141, 142, 143, 144, 145, 146, 147, 148, 149, 150, 151, 152, 153, 154, 155, 156, 157, 158, 159, 160
6. Apply knowledge of language structure and conventions, media techniques, figurative language, and genre to create, critique, and discuss texts.	142, 143, 153, 154
7. Research issues and interests, pose questions, and gather data to communicate discoveries.	141, 143, 149, 152, 153, 154, 155, 157, 158
8. Work with a variety of technological and other resources to collect information and to communicate knowledge.	144, 145, 148, 149
9. Understand and respect the differences in language use across cultures, regions, and social roles.	142, 143, 149, 150, 151, 152, 153, 154, 157, 159, 160
10. Students whose first language is not English use their first language to develop competencies in English and other content areas.	141, 143, 146, 147, 149, 150, 151, 152, 153, 154, 155, 160
11. Participate in a variety of literary communities.	141, 142, 143, 144, 145, 146, 147, 148, 149, 150, 151, 152, 153, 154, 155, 156, 157, 158, 159, 160
12. Use spoken, written, and visual language to accomplish purposes.	141, 142, 143, 144, 145, 146, 147, 148, 149, 150, 151, 152, 153, 154, 155, 156, 157, 158, 159, 160

Social Studies Standards	
1. Culture: Compare similarities and differences between cultures. Describe the importance of cultural unity and diversity.	150, 151, 152, 153, 154, 156, 157, 159, 160
2. Time, Continuity, and Change: Study people, places, and events of the past.	144, 145
3. People, Places, and Environments: Learn about geography and how people interact with the environment.	143, 144, 145, 152, 156, 157, 159, 160
4. Individual Development and Identity: Explore factors that contribute to one's personal identity.	141, 143, 144, 145, 148, 152, 153, 154, 157, 158, 159, 160
5. Individuals, Groups, and Institutions: Identify and describe the roles and influences of various institutions.	149, 157, 159
6. Power, Authority, and Governance: Understand the purpose of government. Describe the rights and responsibilities of individuals and groups.	159
7. Production, Distribution, and Consumption: Explore how people organize to produce, distribute, and consume goods and services.	149
8. Science, Technology, and Society: Describe ways in which science and technology have changed lives.	144, 145
9. Global Connections: Investigate how world societies depend on one another.	149, 159, 160
10. Civic Ideals and Practices: Recognize the functions and ideals of a democratic government. Explain the rights and responsibilities of citizens.	159

Name _____

How Tolerant Are You?

Tolerance is defined as the ability or practice of accepting the race, religion, customs, opinions, or likes of other people; absent of negative prejudice. In other words a tolerant person is someone who respects other people regardless of how they differ from themselves.

Tolerant people:

- stand up for others who are being bullied because of their differences
- take the time to get to know someone before forming an opinion
- see others for how they are alike instead of how they are different
- learn about other cultures to learn to better relate to others
- appreciate and enjoy people who are different
- treat everyone they meet the way that they want to be treated

Use the scale to find out what your tolerance rating is by circling the number in the column that best describes you.

Action of Tolerance	Almost Always	Sometimes	Not Very Often	Never
I stand up for others who are being bullied because they are different.	3	2	1	0
I take the time to get to know someone before I form an opinion of them.	3	2	1	0
I see others for how they are like me instead of how they are different from me.	3	2	1	0
I learn about other cultures so I can relate to them.	3	2	1	0
I appreciate and enjoy people who are different from me.	3	2	1	0
I treat others the way I want to be treated.	3	2	1	0
Totals:				

My total score: _____

How do you rate?

24–20: Master of Tolerance
19–15: Master in Training
14–10: Apprentice
9–5: Beginner
Below 5: Reform Candidate

Name _____

Tolerance is accepting the differences in others without prejudice. Much has been said about tolerance. Read these quotes relating to tolerance. Then work with a partner to decide what each quote means.

You don't live in a world all alone. Your brothers are here, too. —Albert Schweitzer

_____

_____

No one can make you feel inferior without your consent. —Eleanor Roosevelt

_____

_____

Never judge another man until you have walked a mile in his moccasins. —Native American Proverb

_____

_____

Until he extends his circle of compassion to include all living things, man will not himself find peace. —Albert Schweitzer

_____

_____

Give to every human being every right that you claim for yourself. —Robert Ingersoll

_____

_____

Name _____

Tolerance in Action

Your assignment for this activity is to act like a private investigator to observe and find examples of those around you who show tolerance towards others. As you investigate, keep a record of what you see using the log sheet provided.

My Log Sheet

I saw the following act of tolerance demonstrated by _____

_____

_____

_____

I saw the following act of tolerance demonstrated by _____

_____

_____

_____

I saw the following act of tolerance demonstrated by _____

_____

_____

_____

I saw the following act of tolerance demonstrated by _____

_____

_____

_____

The Tolerant Humanitarian

"Man must cease attributing his problems to his environment, and learn to exercise his personal responsibility." The man who spoke these words was Albert Schweitzer. Schweitzer was a doctor, a teacher, an author, an environmentalist, a musician, an anti-nuclear activist, a philosopher, a Nobel Prize winner, a husband, a father, and a friend. But most of all, he was a humanitarian.

Born in Germany, Albert began his interest in the welfare of others when he first entered school. On the first day, he noticed that he was dressed much better than most of his classmates. Arriving at home that afternoon, Albert announced to his parents that he would no longer wear his more expensive clothes to school.

Schweitzer had a natural talent for playing the organ and had decided to become a professional organist. However, he changed those plans at the age of 18 and decided to go into the ministry. He earned his degree and began serving as a pastor and teacher at the local seminary. Schweitzer began to feel that he was not doing enough and began searching for direction when he read an article in a mission magazine. That article described the medical needs of people living in the African Congo. Schweitzer resigned as a pastor and left for medical school.

With his medical degree in hand, Schweitzer persuaded the Paris Missionary Society to send him to Africa. He started a hospital in the only available building, which was an old chicken coop. He began treating the ill. Within nine months, he had treated over two thousand people. When World War I broke out, Schweitzer was sent back to France as a prisoner of war because he was a German citizen in a French-controlled territory. When the war ended, Schweitzer felt drawn back to Africa. He raised the money to return by playing organ concerts across Europe.

After his return to Africa, visitors from around the world, including doctors and the press, came to his jungle hospital to see what he was doing. They found patients sitting in the dust outside the hospital cooking their own meals amongst goats and chickens. These conditions would not have been acceptable anywhere else, but Schweitzer had taken the time to learn the culture. He knew that the Africans wouldn't have stayed in hospital beds and eaten hospital food, so he adapted his service to meet their culture.

Albert Schweitzer received the Nobel Prize for Peace in 1952. He used the money that accompanied the medal to build a new building in his hospital camp for lepers. Albert Schweitzer was a great humanitarian whose actions demonstrated his tolerance as he worked selflessly for others.

Name _____

The Tolerant Humanitarian

What do you think Albert Schweitzer meant by the quote at the beginning of the story?

_____

_____

How did Albert Schweitzer show tolerance towards his fellow man as a child? As an adult?

_____

_____

Why do you think that Albert Schweitzer has often been called the world's greatest humanitarian?

_____

_____

Would you consider Albert Schweitzer a good choice for a biographical sketch of a personality on tolerance? Why or why not?

_____

_____

Nobel Prizes are awarded to people and/or organizations whose contributions make our world a better place. Pair up with a partner and brainstorm possibilities for a prize that could be awarded for acts of tolerance.

- Decide what your prize should be called. What are the criteria for winning your prize?

- Decide on the monetary amount that should accompany such an award.

- Carefully choose your first winner of the award.

- Prepare a short summary to make to the other members of your class based on the above direction.

The Boy Who Saw in Color

This science fiction story reminds us that although we may differ from someone else we can appreciate and enjoy those differences.

Cast:

narrator	classmate #1
boy	classmate #2
boy's mother	classmate #3
boy's teacher	

Setting: *A planet in our Universe that is much like Earth*

Narrator: On a planet far from Earth, there is a race of people like us except that they only have one eye. This is the story of a boy who is born on their planet with two eyes and how he is treated on his first day of school.

Boy's mother: *(Walking with him to school)* I'm sure that you're going to love school.

Boy: I'm worried that the other kids will make fun of me because I am different and I can't see like they can.

Boy's mother: *(Arriving at school)* Don't worry! We're all different in some ways. I'll see you after school.

Boy's teacher: Welcome, class! Find the seat with your name on it and then put your things in your desk.

Classmate #1: Look at that kid. He has two eyes, I'm not sitting by him.

Classmate #2: My parents said I'm not supposed to get near him either.

Classmate #3: I'll be happy to sit by him because I've been waiting to meet him.

Boy's teacher: Thank you, and as for you, two, I'll see you during recess.

Narrator: The morning was filled with first day business until it was finally time for recess.

Classmate #3: *(To the boy)* I heard that you see things that I can't. Is that true?

Name _____

Boy: Well, I can't see far, far away like you can, and I can't see very well in the dark like you can. But I can see things in color.

Classmate #3: What is color? I can only see in black and white.

Boy: Color is amazing. It makes everything so bright. Instead of looking out the window and seeing a gray yard with a gray sky, I see a green yard filled with red and yellow flowers covered by a blue sky.

Classmate #3: That sounds beautiful. I wish that I could see the way that you see.

Boy: And I've always wished that I could see the way that you see.

Classmate #3: But everyone sees the way I see so there's nothing really special about me the way there is about you.

Boy: I've never looked at it that way. I just always thought I was different.

Classmate #3: You are different, but it is your difference that makes you special.

Narrator: The boys continued to talk and work throughout the day until the bell rings to dismiss class. The boy's mother is waiting for him and together they walk home and discuss his day.

Boy's mother: How was your first day?

Boy: At first no one wanted to sit by me and they all looked at me funny, but then one boy said that he had been waiting to meet me. We sat by each other in class and talked during recess. He says that having two eyes makes me special.

Boy's mother: You are special, but I think that your new friend must be special, too.

Boy: Oh, he is. Can I invite him over to play tomorrow?

Boy's mother: I think that that would be a great idea.

Narrator: So the next afternoon, the two boys got together and discovered that they were more alike than they were different. The friendship they forged that first day deepened as they grew older and understood one another better.

What is the lesson to be learned from this play? Discuss your answer with other members of your class.

_____

_____

_____

Name _____

Writing About Tolerance

Tolerance is respecting others for their differences without prejudice. Your assignment is to pair up with a partner and use a dictionary and a thesaurus to help you learn more about the word *tolerance*.

Combine your research and jot down words and phrases that help to better define the word.

_____

_____

_____

How is being prejudiced towards someone different than not liking that person?

_____

_____

How do you think people become prejudiced? _____

_____

_____

What is respect?_____

_____

_____

What are some differences that we need to be tolerant of in today's changing world?

_____

_____

How can you show someone that you respect his or her differences?

_____

_____

Both you and your partner should exchange conversation about times when you were both tolerant of others. Then describe those actions on the lines below.

_____

_____

_____

If the Earth Had a Population of 100 . . .

What would the earth be like if we could shrink its population from over 6 billion people to a single small village of a hundred people? In this activity, you will work with a partner or within a small group to solve these simple math problems to help you to answer this question. Then you will create a poster to let others learn about your findings. Remember that each equation must equal 100. Make your poster as attractive as you can.

If the Earth were a village of 100 people:

A. 70 of the people would be non-white and _____ would be white.

B. 32 of the people would be children and _____ would be adults.

C. 52 of the people would be female and _____ would be male.

D. 7 people would have cars, but _____ people would not.

F. 1 person would have a computer, but _____ would not.

G. 70 people would be non-Christian and _____ would be Christian.

H. 61 of the people would be Asian, 13 African, 12 European,

　　1 from the South Pacific, and _____ from North and South America.

I. 50 of the people in the village would speak languages broken down as follows:

　　17 would speak Chinese, 8 would speak Hindi and Urdu, 6 would speak Spanish,

　　6 would speak Russian, 4 would speak Arabic, _____ would speak English, and

　　the other 50 people would speak one of over 200 different languages,

J. 75 of the people have some supply of food and shelter, but _____ do not.

K. Of the energy in this village 20 people consume 80%, and _____ share the remaining 20%

L. In one year, 1 person in the village will die, but in the same year 2 babies will

　　be born so that at the year's end there will be _____ people in the village.

Tolerant Role-Plays

Tolerant people accept the differences of others without prejudice. Because we are all unique individuals, everyone differs from everyone else in some way. If we focus on how we are all alike instead of getting caught up in how we are all different, the world would be a much more peaceful place. Pair up with a partner and look at each of the following role-play situations. Then decide the steps that should be taken to show tolerance in each situation. With your partner, choose one of these situations and create a short skit you will present to the other members of your class.

Terrance and the New Boy

Terrance's teacher has asked him to be a buddy for the new boy that will be joining their class the next day. She explains to Terrance that the new boy is in a wheelchair because he was paralyzed in a skateboarding accident. Terrance is an avid skateboarder, but is worried that he won't know what to say to the new boy to make him feel welcome.

Ariel Volunteers

Ariel's mother has arranged for her to volunteer one afternoon at the local retirement home. Ariel tells her mother that the place smells funny and that the older residents scare her. Her mother insists that she go.

Herbie Joins the Team

Herbie has a new artificial leg. He has always dreamed of playing soccer and can't wait to join a team. His new leg allows him to run and kick just like all of the other boys on the team. Herbie is worried that the team will not want him.

Bianca and the Girl Next Door

Bianca watches as a moving van unloads furniture to the house next door. She gets excited when she sees a girl about her age coming out of the house. Bianca is about to go over and introduce herself, but stops when she hears the girl speaking to her mother in a foreign language.

Simon and the Christmas Party

Simon's family does not celebrate Christmas. Simon is not allowed to participate in the class Christmas party. Simon feels left out and different.

Option Role-Play

Suppose you and your partner have a better idea for a role-play scenario that will demonstrate your understanding of the concept of tolerance. If you want to create your own, simply choose a name for your role-play and create dialogue that will follow the same procedure of those above. Then share your role-play with other members of your class.

Name _____

School-to-Home Connection

One of the steps towards tolerance is learning about the cultures of others. Our culture is defined by the traditions we hold, the holidays we celebrate, the foods we eat, and the practices we pass along from one generation to the next. Take this assignment home and discuss the questions with other family members. Jot down your findings and return the paper to your class where you can share it with other classmates.

What foods do you and your family members consider "quite common" for family meals in your home?

_____

_____

Which holidays, celebrations, and ceremonies are most important to your family?

_____

_____

What family traditions does your family follow? How did the tradition originate in your family? (Example: eating black-eyed peas on New Years for good luck) Remember that family traditions help to make each family unique.

_____

_____

What practices or customs have been passed down to you from other generations?

_____

_____

Are there any television shows that you watch on a regular basis as a family? If so, which ones?

_____

_____

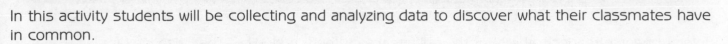

In this activity students will be collecting and analyzing data to discover what their classmates have in common.

Materials: slips of paper or index cards for each student, student page, blank sheet of legal-sized paper, colored pencils and/or markers

1. Write the following statements on the board.
   - No one is exactly like me.
   - I have many things in common with the members of my family, community, and classmates.
   - Every person in the world needs some of the same things I need.

2. Ask students to share ideas that support these statements.

3. Remind students that tolerant people focus on how they are like others. Then ask them to come up with some questions they could ask their fellow classmates to find out more about how they are alike.

Example Questions: What is your favorite fast food restaurant? What is your favorite holiday? What is your favorite subject in school? What is your favorite television program? What is your favorite color?, etc.

4. Write the student questions on the board and then have students choose which questions they think will tell them the most about their classmates.

5. Distribute the index cards or slips of paper and have each student write both the question and their answer on a different card or slip of paper.

6. Distribute student pages. Then divide students into groups of three or four students each, and assign each group a question.

7. Have students write their assigned question on the designated line. Then they fill in the grid using their classmate's question cards

8. Have students make their graphs and share their results with the rest of the class.

Name _____

Tolerant people respect others for their differences without prejudice. They also look for ways that they are like someone else. In this activity, you will be collecting and reporting data taken in a survey.

Materials: Colored pencils, markers, ruler, and legal-sized piece of blank paper

1. Divide your group's cards according to the question asked.

2. Have one member of your group go to the other groups to get your group's question cards.

3. Tally the data from your group's cards in the table below.

Our Group's Question: _____

Student's Answer	Number of Answers

4. Use the legal-sized paper and your markers to make a graph that depicts your results.

5. Title your graph with your group's question

6. Write and complete the following conclusion below your graph:

   Most of our classmates _____

7. Add illustrations to make your graph attractive and place on bulletin board with those of other groups.

Name _____

Don't Label Me!

Labels are used to classify groups of objects or things and to provide information. Some labels are helpful, but others can be harmful. Continue working with your group to examine the label on a can.

Materials: one canned good, this student page

1. Use the label on your canned good to complete the table

2. Answer the questions to consider

What's On Our Label?

Information to look for	What's on the label
Name of Product	
Number of Ounces	
Brand	
Serving Size	
Servings Per Container	
Calories	
Colors on Label	

Questions to consider:

1. How does the label on a product help you?

   _____

2. Can you be completely sure that the can contains what the label says it does

   without opening the can? _____ WHY or WHY NOT? _____

   _____

3. Product labels are based on what is inside the can. What are some labels we use to label people and on what basis are these labels often made?

   _____

   _____

4. Do you think that labels we use for people are helpful or harmful?

   _____

   _____

Name _____

Long ago in a distant land, six blind men lived together. All of them had heard of elephants, but they had never seen one. When they heard that an elephant and his trainer would be visiting their village, they couldn't wait to actually visit this beast that they had heard so much about. They made their way to the place where the elephant was being kept and then each blind man touched the elephant and relayed his observation to the others. The first man touched the elephant's side and concluded that an elephant is like a wall. The second man touched the elephant's trunk and exclaimed that an elephant is like a snake. The third man touched the elephant's tusk and stated that an elephant is like a spear. The fourth blind man touched the elephant's leg and decided that an elephant is like a tree. The fifth man touched the elephant's ear and proclaimed that an elephant is like a fan. The last man touched the elephant's tail and said that an elephant is like a rope.

Questions to consider:

Did all of the blind men relay the same observations? _____
Why or Why Not?

_____

_____

What is the moral of this tale?

_____

_____

You will be given a single piece of a 100-piece puzzle to observe and use your observations in drawing conclusions .

Draw a sketch of your puzzle piece in the space provided.

What do you think the finished puzzle probably looks like?

According to your teacher, what does the finished puzzle really look like?

Do you think that it is important to take the time to see the picture on the box of the completed puzzle before making any conclusions about the location of any specific piece? How does this relate to our study of becoming more tolerant?

_____

_____

_____

Name _____

Craig Kielburger is a Canadian youth who founded *Free the Children*, an organization whose goal is to free children in Third World countries who have been sold into slave labor. Many students across the country have joined his effort and have contributed to this cause. Today, Craig and his organization are responsible for freeing thousands of children who now go to one of the 300 schools that were built with money raised. Craig has shown tolerance in many different ways. In this activity you will read more about Craig and then reflect and write about times that you have acted like Craig.

Kielburger shows tolerance by standing up for children who cannot stand on their own. Write about a time that you stood up for someone who was being bullied because they were different.

_____

_____

Kielburger realizes that children all over the world are like him in that we all need some of the same things. Write about some of the things that we all need.

_____

_____

Kielburger often travels to different countries so that he can meet with and talk to the children he is trying to help. He takes the time to get to know them and to learn about their cultures. Write about a time that you took the time to get to know someone whose culture was different than your own.

_____

_____

Kielburger's goal is that children all over the world will be treated the way that he would like to be treated. Write about a time that you treated someone the way that you wanted to be treated.

_____

_____

Name _____

My Personal Tolerance Log Sheet

Steps towards Tolerance	Example of a time I showed this step
Standing up for others who are being bullied because they are different	
Taking the time to get to know someone before I form an opinion about that person	
Focusing on how others are like me instead of how they are different	
Learning about other's cultures and practices	
Making friends with people who are different me	
Treating others the way that I would like to be treated	

0-7682-2795-X *Character Education*

Declaration of Tolerance

Objective: To provide students with an opportunity to discuss and create a classroom declaration to help students become more tolerant.

Materials: Poster board, colored markers, UN's Declaration on the Rights of a Child, and p. 141

1. Provide students with a copy of both p. 141 and the UN's Declaration of Rights shown below. Discuss each page as a class, and then divide students into groups.

2. Have students work within small groups to develop their own Declaration of Tolerance to be posted on your bulletin board.

The United Nations' Declaration on the Rights of a Child

The Right to affection, love, and understanding

The Right to adequate nutrition and medical care

The Right to free medical care

The Right to full opportunity for play and recreation

The Right to a name and nationality

The Right to special care, if handicapped

The Right to be among the first to receive relief in times of disaster

The Right to be a useful member of society and to develop individual abilities

The Right to be brought up in a spirit of peace and universal brotherhood

The Right to enjoy these rights, regardless of race, color, sex, religion, national or social origin

---

Questions to Discuss: What is tolerance? How do we show tolerance? What is the UN's Job? Why do we have a UN?

Sharing Family Culture

Objective: To provide students with an opportunity to share information about their family's culture.

Materials: Student interview p. 152, colored paper, markers, scissors, glue

Procedure: Have students create a quilt square that communicates their culture, then connect and display completed squares.

Questions to Discuss: What is culture? What defines culture?

Tolerance in Seuss

Objective: To provide students with an opportunity to evaluate and interpret literature.

Materials: Dr. Seuss Books: *The Sneetches*, *The Pale Green Pants*, *Horton Hears a Who*, *Green Eggs and Ham*, *The Butter Battle Book*, and *Thadwick, the Big Hearted Moose*.

Procedure:

1. Discuss with the students the concept of a moral.

2. Divide students into groups of three to four students each and provide each group with one of the Dr. Seuss books.

3. Students read the book and then create a poster for the book that communicates the book's name and the moral of the story as it relates to tolerance.

Extension: Students can also write and perform a Reader's Theater for younger grades or for the rest of their class.

Questions to Discuss: What is the moral of each book? How do the morals differ? How are they the same?

International Pen Pals

Objective: To provide students with an opportunity to learn more about another country through letter writing.

Procedure:

1. Use the Internet to find a class to adopt in another country.

2. Assign students to research the country where their adoptive class lives.

3. Have students exchange letters with their adoptive class over an extended period of time.

Questions to Discuss: How are the students in both classes the same? How do the students in both classes differ? How does the country we live in affect who we are?

Perseverance

The activities in this unit are designed to help teach perseverance. *Perseverance* is defined as steadfastness in seeking a goal. Once you set a goal, you keep on going even when you may feel like doing otherwise. Goal setting is the first step towards perseverance. Helping students understand the importance of setting goals, then creating a plan to reach those goals, and finally remaining committed to that plan is a part of being a good teacher.

The first teacher extension; *I Can Folder*, is an excellent springboard to begin the unit. Student activity pages include writing activities, reader's theater, role-playing activities, and hands-on activities. They are provided to allow students to identify and internalize the traits and behaviors associated with perseverance.

Materials needed and teacher set-up time is minimal to allow you more time to teach. All activities and extensions provided in this book are directly related to the IRA/NCTE and NCSS Standards as outlined on the next page. Below is a sample note that can be copied and sent home with students to introduce their parents and caregivers to this unit and to encourage them to participate with their child.

Dear Parent or Guardian:

Our class is working to build good character. In this unit we are working on perseverance. We have defined perseverance as steadfastness in seeking a goal. We have also outlined some important actions that will help us to persevere: setting realistic goals; creating a plan to meet our goals; solving problems when our plan encounters difficulties; surrounding ourselves with people who encourage and support us; and committing ourselves to never give up.

Since perseverance is needed both at home and in the classroom, we ask that you discuss with your child their goals. You can help them to identify ways that they can persevere and eventually achieve their goals. We also ask that you commend your child when you "catch them" demonstrating perseverance to reach a goal.

During this unit, we will also be sending home an activity to be done with your family. Working together, we can help your child to become committed to achieving his or her goals. Thank you for your support and the positive role model that you provide to your child.

Sincerely,

_____

Standards Correlation

English Language Arts Standards	Page Numbers
1. Read a wide range of texts.	163, 166, 167, 170, 171, 172, 173, 175, 176, 177, 179
2. Read a wide range of literature.	164, 168, 169, 178, 182
3. Apply a variety of strategies to comprehend and interpret texts.	163, 164, 166, 167, 168, 169, 170, 171, 172, 173, 178, 179, 182
4. Use spoken, written, and visual language to communicate effectively.	163, 164, 165, 166, 167, 168, 169, 170, 171, 172, 173, 174, 175, 176, 177, 178, 179, 180
5. Use a variety of strategies while writing and use elements of the writing process to communicate.	163, 164, 165, 166, 167, 168, 169, 170, 171, 172, 173, 174, 175, 176, 177, 178, 179, 180
6. Apply knowledge of language structure and conventions, media techniques, figurative language, and genre to create, critique, and discuss texts.	164, 165, 166, 167, 168, 169, 172, 173, 182
7. Research issues and interests, pose questions, and gather data to communicate discoveries.	163, 165, 166, 167, 171, 174, 175, 176, 177
8. Work with a variety of technological and other resources to collect information and to communicate knowledge.	166, 167, 171, 175, 176, 177
9. Understand and respect the differences in language use across cultures, regions, and social roles.	164, 172, 173, 174, 175, 176, 177, 182
10. Students whose first language is not English use their first language to develop competencies in English and other content areas.	163, 164, 165, 170, 171, 172, 173, 174, 178
11. Participate in a variety of literary communities.	163, 164, 165, 166, 167, 170, 171, 172, 173, 174, 175, 176, 177, 178, 179, 180
12. Use spoken, written, and visual language to accomplish purposes.	163, 164, 165, 166, 167. 170. 171, 174, 175, 176, 177, 178, 179, 180, 182

Social Studies Standards	
1. Culture: Compare similarities and differences between cultures. Describe the importance of cultural unity and diversity.	168, 169, 174, 179
2. Time, Continuity, and Change: Study people, places, and events of the past.	166, 167, 171, 174
3. People, Places, and Environments: Learn about geography and how people interact with the environment.	165, 168, 169, 171, 174, 179
4. Individual Development and Identity: Explore factors that contribute to one's personal identity.	163, 164, 165, 166, 167, 170, 171, 174, 179, 180, 182
5. Individuals, Groups, and Institutions: Identify and describe the roles and influences of various institutions.	175, 176, 177, 179
6. Power, Authority, and Governance: Understand the purpose of government. Describe the rights and responsibilities of individuals and groups.	
7. Production, Distribution, and Consumption: Explore how people organize to produce, distribute, and consume goods and services.	
8. Science, Technology, and Society: Describe ways in which science and technology have changed lives.	166, 167, 175, 176, 177
9. Global Connections: Investigate how world societies depend on one another.	179
10. Civic Ideals and Practices: Recognize the functions and ideals of a democratic government. Explain the rights and responsibilities of citizens.	165, 175, 176, 177

Name _____

Perseverance is defined as steadfastness in seeking a goal. This means that once you set a goal, you keep working at it until you have reached that goal.

People who persevere . . .
- set realistic goals for themselves.
- make a plan to reach their goal.
- problem-solve if their plan does not work.
- give their best to everything they do.
- surround themselves with people who support and encourage them .
- evaluate how their actions affect their goals.
- check and reward the progress they are making towards reaching their goals.
- don't give up even when things get tough.

Use the scale to find out what your perseverance rating is by circling the number in the column that best describes you.

Cooperation Action	Almost Always	Sometimes	Not Very Often	Never
I set realistic goals for myself.	3	2	1	0
I make plans to reach my goals.	3	2	1	0
I problem-solve to change my plan if it doesn't work.	3	2	1	0
I give my best to everything I do.	3	2	1	0
I surround myself with people who encourage and support me.	3	2	1	0
I evaluate how my actions affect my goals.	3	2	1	0
I check and reward the progress I am making toward my goals.	3	2	1	0
I don't give up, even when things get tough.	3	2	1	0
Totals:				

My total score: _____

How do you rate?

    24–20: Master of Cooperation
    19–15: Master in Training
    14–10: Apprentice in Cooperation
      9–5: Beginner
  Below 5: Reform Candidate

 0-7682-2795-X *Character Education*

Name _____

Much has been said about perseverance. In this activity, you will read some quotes related to perseverance and then work with your partner or group to write what you think they mean in your own words.

Ninety percent of the failures come from people who have the habit of making excuses.
—George Washington Carver

Your words _____

Perseverance is not a long race; it is many short races one after another. —Walter Elliott

Your words _____

I am a slow walker, but I never walk backward. —Abraham Lincoln

Your words _____

Mistakes are the doorway to discovery. —Sam Horn

Your words _____

We can do anything we want to do if we stick to it long enough. —Helen Keller

Your words _____

Perseverance and failure cannot coexist. —Unknown

Your words _____

Obstacles cannot crush me, for every obstacle yields to stern resolve. —Leonardo de Vinci

Your words _____

Link yourself to your potential, not to your past. —Stephen Covey

Your words _____

Mistakes are the doorway to discovery. —Sam Horn

         0-7682-2795-X *Character Education*

Name _____

Observing Perseverance

People who persevere are all around you. Consider the first grader who is persevering to learn to read. Other examples of perseverance are also right in front of you. In this activity, acting as a private eye, you will log examples of how and what other people are doing to achieve their goals in different locations.

I saw someone in my neighborhood working to persevere at _____

_____ by _____

_____

I saw someone in my school working to persevere at _____

_____ by _____

_____

I read about someone working to persevere at _____

_____ by _____

_____

I saw someone on television demonstrating perseverance by _____

_____ by _____

_____

I saw someone in my town working to persevere at _____

_____ by _____

_____

The Man with Bright Ideas

The invention of the light bulb illuminated our world and made it possible for homes to replace dangerous gaslights with more efficient electric ones. The story of how the light bulb made its way into your living room is one of perseverance. The man who made it all possible overcame many obstacles and refused to give up until he had reached his goal. During his lifetime, he patented over 1,000 different inventions designed to make life easier. By volume, through variety, and with the impact of his inventions, Thomas Edison made it seem that nothing was beyond our reach. If we work hard enough and believe in our ability to succeed, we will succeed.

Edison was born on February 11, 1847 in Milan, Ohio. He attended public school for a very short time because his teachers reported that he was a dull, unintelligent child. In response, his mother home-schooled him and encouraged him to pursue his interests. His interests included reading and chemistry. At the age of 10, Edison began working as a train boy at the local train yard. He used an empty train car to house his chemistry lab and to publish his own newspaper. While at the railroad, Edison became fascinated by the telegraph, a device that made it possible to transmit messages from one place to another. His fascination led him to his first invention, a telegraph repeating instrument that could transmit messages automatically. Edison's success enabled him to leave the train yard and begin a career as a full-time inventor at the age of 22.

Edison's first patent was for a voting machine. Although no one wanted to buy it, Edison did not consider it a failure saying, "Every wrong attempt discarded is a step forward." With this mindset, Edison surged forward and developed hundreds of inventions over the next few years. His most famous, the incandescent light bulb, was unveiled in 1879.

Incandescent light bulbs create light by using electricity to heat a thin strip of filament until it glows. This filament is inside in a glass bulb that contains no air. The problem Edison and his associates faced was determining the material to use for the filament. Thousands of different materials for the filament were tried, but they all burned up too quickly. By chance, an Edison employee named Lewis Latimer discovered that a carbonized cotton thread worked well. After working for over a year, Edison's company produced and marketed a 16-watt bulb that burned for 1500 hours.

Thomas Edison died on October 18, 1931 at the age of 84. Three days later all the electric lights in the United States were dimmed for one minute to honor the man who believed in setting and reaching goals to change the world.

Name _____

Questions from the Biography

What are some obstacles that Thomas Edison overcame during his lifetime?

_____

_____

What do you think Edison meant when he said, "Every wrong attempt discarded is a step forward"?

_____

_____

Why do you think that all of the electric lights were dimmed for one minute to honor Edison after his death?

_____

_____

Edison received over 1,000 patents during his lifetime. Use research books and/or the Internet to find out about some of them and record your research to be shared with other members of your class.

Invention— _____

How it changed our world— _____

Invention— _____

How it changed our world— _____

Invention— _____

How it changed our world— _____

Invention— _____

How it changed our world— _____

The Hero of Holland

In this Dutch tale we see a young boy with firm resolve work selflessly to achieve his goal despite pain, fear, and the elements.

Cast:

Narrator   Peter's Mother   A Man
Peter: a Little Dutch Boy   Hans: A Blind Man   The Crowd
Peter's Father   Passerby

The Setting: *A small village in Holland by the North Sea*

Narrator: Holland is a country where much of the land lies below sea level. Because of this, great walls known as dikes were built to keep the North Sea from rushing in and flooding the land. All of the people knew how important the dikes were to their village. This is the story of one boy's goal to save the village.

Peter: Is it okay if I walk over to see my friend Hans today? It's been some time since I've visited him, and I'm afraid he might be lonely.

Peter's Father: It is okay with me as long as you're home before dark.

Narrator: Peter's father then headed to work and Peter went to see his friend.

Hans: *(Turning his head towards a sound)* Peter? Is that you?

Peter: Yes, Hans I am so happy to see you. How have you been?

Hans: I've been a little lonely, I'm so glad that you are here. It smells like we may be getting a storm later this evening. I hope that the dikes are secure.

Peter: I think you're right about the storm, I saw dark clouds off to the west as I was crossing the bridge. Don't worry about the dikes. I'll be sure to check them on my way home.

Narrator: So Peter visited with his friend until it was time for him to head home.

Peter: I better get going as I promised my father I'd be home before dark. I'll be sure to check the dikes on my way. I'll visit again soon.

Narrator: Peter checked the dikes as he promised. He noticed a small break in one of the walls and moved in closer for a better view.

Peter: This looks bad. I must find a way to block the water before it weakens the wall and floods the village. I think my finger is the right size.

Narrator: So Peter plugged the break with his finger and called for help.

Perseverance requires that you set a goal and then work without quitting to reach it. In this activity, you will use a formula to set a short-term goal based on your abilities.

Title one side of your blank paper "Abilities." Then brainstorm and write down all of the things that you do well both at home and school.

Turn your paper over and title this side "Possible goals." Then brainstorm and write down a list of things you would like to do better.

Look at the goal-setting formula below. Then use both your lists to create a goal based on your abilities.

Write down your goal and then complete the statements about your goal.

Goal setting Formula: When setting a goal consider the following:

Specific—Is your goal clearly stated so that anyone can understand it?
Measurable—Can your goal be measured and tracked?
Achievable—Can your goal be reached with your abilities?
Relevant—Why are you making this goal and how will it help you?
Thinkable—Can you make and carry out a plan to reach your goal?

My short-term goal for this year is to _____

_____

I plan to measure and track the progress I am making towards my goal by _____

_____

The abilities that I have that will help me reach
this goal are _____

_____

Reaching this goal will help me now by _____

_____

I will work to persevere in reaching this goal by

_____

Setting Goals

Peter: Help me! Please, Help me!

Narrator: Sadly, Peter's cries were carried away into the darkening night by the wind. Meanwhile, at home, Peter's mother and father became worried and decided to go looking for him.

Peter's Mother: *(calling out over the storm)* Peter? Peter? Where are you?

Passerby: Can I help you, Miss?

Peter's Mother: Yes, my son Peter went to visit his friend Hans across the bridge, and he hasn't returned home yet. I'm worried that this storm will wash him away.

Passerby: Don't worry. I know Hans and he would have your son stay with him until the storm has passed. Why don't you head home before this storm gets worse?

Peter's Mother: You are probably right. I think I will head home.

Narrator: Meanwhile Peter could hear his mother calling over the noise of the storm, but his cries back to her were not heard over the sounds of the storm.

Peter: *(Calling out)* Mother! Mother! I'm over here! I need help! Mother! Mother?

Narrator: As the storm worsened, Peter realized that no one else would come. He placed his jacket over his head and remained steadfast through the stormy night. The next morning a man going to work heard a groan.

Man: *(approaching Peter)* Are you hurt? Are you lost? Do you need help?

Peter: Yes, there is a break in the wall and I have worked all night to plug it with my finger, but I fear I cannot hold out much longer. Please sound the alarm and alert the villagers to come help.

Narrator: So the man rushed off to sound the alarm, alerting the villagers.

Crowd: *(to Peter)* You are so brave to have stayed here all night and save our village! What can we do to repay you?

Peter: Just help me home, as I know my parents are worried.

Narrator: So the crowd carried Peter home and told his parents of the brave deed he had done. To this day everyone remembers the bravery and perseverance of the little boy who stopped the angry waters of the North Sea through a stormy night with nothing more than his finger and courage.

Name _____

Inventing Perseverance

In this activity you will use research books and/or the Internet to find out how each person persevered to invent or discover something that changed the world. Then, you will decide how this discovery or invention made an impact. Underline the word discovered or invented. The first one has been done for you.

Edward Jenner <u>discovered</u> or invented a smallpox vaccine
Impact—A life threatening disease can now be prevented

Joseph Lister discovered or invented _____

Impact— _____

Alexander Fleming discovered or invented _____

Impact— _____

Henry Ford discovered or invented _____

Impact— _____

The Wright Brothers discovered or invented _____

Impact— _____

Louis Pasteur discovered or invented _____

Impact— _____

Mary Anderson discovered or invented _____

Impact— _____

Florence Nightingale discovered or invented _____

Impact— _____

Name _____

Roles of Perseverance

Perseverance often requires that we overcome obstacles by solving problems to reach our goals. In this activity, you will decide what each person can do to show perseverance towards reaching his/her goal, then write down, and role-play your decision.

Steps to help you persevere and **reach** a goal:
Remind yourself of the goal you set.
Encourage yourself to do your best.
Ask others who support you for help.
Check and reward your progress.
Have a plan of action and then problem solve to change it.

Juan's favorite TV show will be on in ten minutes. His bedtime is right after the show. He still has a lot of homework to complete before he goes to bed. Juan wants to do both, but knows that he cannot.

A way in which Juan can show perseverance is _____
_____

Sally's friends have invited her to go roller-blading with them. She has tried other sports and is not very good at them. Sally really wants to spend time with her friends but is afraid that she will not be very good at roller-blading.

A way in which Sally can show perseverance is _____
_____
_____
_____

_____

William has a problem reading because he is dyslexic and words get turned around. He has a book report due in a few days and has not started reading his book yet because it is very hard for him to make sense of what he reads.

A way in which William can show perseverance is _____
_____
_____
_____
_____

Name _____

Roles of Perseverance

Vanessa had a big fight with her mom before she left for school. She has an important test today and wants to make a good grade

A way in which Vanessa can show perseverance is_____
_____

Phillip has been very sick. He has missed a week of school. Phillip's grades are very important to him. When he goes back to school, he knows that he will have a lot of work to catch up on.

A way in which Phillip can show perseverance is _____
_____

Felicia has been working very hard to learn a new piece of music to play at her recital. She has been practicing every night for an hour. The recital is Saturday afternoon and Felicia still has a hard time with one section of the music.

A way in which Felicia can show perseverance is_____
_____

Orlando loves to play basketball. He tried out for the school team last year and did not make it. He has been practicing every day for the past year, but is afraid to try out again this year.

A way in which Orlando can show perseverance is _____
_____
_____
_____
_____

Allison has been saving her money to buy a new bike she wants. On her way home, she sees that the new CD she has been waiting for is out. Allison really wants the CD, but has been saving for months to get the bike.

A way that Allison can show perseverance is _____
_____
_____
_____

   0-7682-2795-X *Character Education*

Name _____

School-to-Home Connection

The members of your family have all had to persevere to reach a goal. In this activity, use the newspaper format of *Who, What, When, Where, Why*, and *How* to interview someone in your family about a time that they showed perseverance. Share your findings with other members of your class.

_____

_____

_____

_____

_____

_____

_____

_____

_____

_____

_____

_____

_____

Perseverance Across America—Teacher Page

Divide students into pairs and assign a different person from the list below to each pair. Students then research the personality and prepare a report to be shared with other members of the class using the format on the student pages. The report page should include a drawing of the personality's accomplishments.

People to choose from:

Person	Birth State	Accomplishment
Christopher Reeve	New York	Paralyzed actor-director
Dr. Charles Drew	Washington D.C.	Discovered blood plasma
Sequoyah	Georgia	Wrote the Cherokee Alphabet
Jesse Owens	Alabama	Olympic athlete
Walt Disney	Illinois	Animator and amusement parks
Jim Abbott	Michigan	One armed pitcher
Helen Keller	Alabama	Blind and deaf educator
Garrett A. Morgan	Kentucky	Inventor: gas mask and traffic light
Sally Ride	California	Astronaut
Ellen Ochoa	California	Astronaut
Sidney Portier	Florida	Academy award winning actor
Benjamin Banneker	Maryland	Mathematician and inventor
Granville T. Woods	Ohio	Inventor
Susan B. Anthony	Massachusetts	Women's rights activist
Harriet Tubman	Maryland	Underground railroad
Rachel Carson	Pennsylvania	Environmentalist
Vicki Manalo Draves	California	Olympic diver
Jonas Salk	New York	Discovered Polio vaccine
Robert Goddard	Massachusetts	Invented liquid fuel rockets
Jim Henson	Mississippi	Invented the Muppets
Willis Carrier	New York	Invented central air conditioning
Stephen Bechtel	Indiana	Architect
Thomas Watson, Jr.	Ohio	Developed IBM computers
Ray Kroc	Illinois	Founder of McDonalds
Jackie Robinson	Georgia	First black baseball player
Franklin D. Roosevelt	New York	Paralyzed president
Martin Luther King Jr.	Georgia	Civil-rights activist
John Glenn	Ohio	Astronaut
Matthew Henson	Maryland	Arctic Explorer
Edwin Land	Connecticut	Invented Polaroid camera
Stevie Wonder	Michigan	Blind musician
Babe Zaharius	Texas	Olympic athlete

Name _____

Perseverance Across the USA: Student Note Page

Use research books and/or the Internet to complete the note outline for the person your teacher has assigned to you and your partner.

Use your note sheet to complete the report page for the person you researched to include the following:

- Write a headline that tells what goals your personality reached to achieve success.
- Draw a colored picture that shows your personality or their accomplishment.
- Write an article that includes all of the information in your note sheet.

Personality— _____

_____

Goals set by this person— _____

_____

_____

_____

Difficulties endured to accomplish goals— _____

_____

_____

Describe how this personality can be identified as a person showing perseverance—

_____

_____

What accomplishment places this personality in the category of "those to be remembered?"

_____

_____

Name _____

_____

Headline

Name _____

It Couldn't Be Done

By Edgar A. Guest

Somebody said that it couldn't be done,
But he with a chuckle replied
That maybe it couldn't, but he would be one
Who wouldn't say so till he'd tried.

So he buckled right in with a trace of a grin
On his face. If he worried, he hid it.
He started to sing as he tackled the thing
That couldn't be done, and he did it.

Somebody scoffed: "Oh, you'll never do that;
At least no one has ever done it."
But he took off his coat and he took off his hat,
And the first thing we knew, he'd begun it.

With a lift of his chin and a bit of a grin,
Without any doubting or quidbit,
He started to sing as he tackled the thing
That couldn't be done and he did it.

There are thousands to tell you it cannot be done,
There are thousands to prophesy failure;
There are thousands to point out to you, one by one,
The dangers that wait to assail you.

But just buckle in with a bit of a grin,
Just take off your coat and go to it;
Just start to sing as you tackle the thing
That "cannot be done", and you'll do it.

What does this poem mean to you? _____

_____

Think of a time in our history when someone said that something could not be done and then
someone went out and did it. Remember: They said that Columbus would fall off the edge of the
world if he tried to sail to the New World.

_____

_____

Name _____

Reflections on Perseverance

In this activity, you will read examples of how others have persevered then reflect and write about times that you have persevered under the same circumstances.

Craig Kielburger is a Canadian youth who founded Free the Children, an organization whose goal is to free children in third world countries who have been sold into slave labor. Many students across the country have joined his effort and have contributed to this cause. Today, Craig and his organization are responsible for freeing thousands of children who now go to one of the 300 schools that were built with money raised. Write about a time that you enlisted the help of others to persevere and reach one of your goals:

_____

_____

_____

Dr. Seuss was told by his High School art teacher to stay away from any profession that had to do with art. His fraternity brothers in college voted him "Least likely to succeed." His first book, Dr. Seuss's ABC's was rejected by all of the publishers he took it to. Seuss did not listen to others and went on to become the best-loved children's author. Write about a time that you did not listen to others who tried to discourage you from attempting one of your goals.

_____

_____

_____

Doctors told Wilma Rudolf that she would never walk due to a shrunken left leg caused from polio and other childhood illnesses. Wilma refused to accept this verdict and became the first woman to win three Olympic gold medals. She won the 100-meter dash, the 200-meter dash, and was a member of the 4 x 100-meter relay. Write about a time that you overcame something to persevere and reach a goal.

_____

_____

_____

_____

Name _____

My Personal Perseverance Log Sheet

Perseverance Action:	Example of a time I showed this action
Setting goals that you can reach	
Making a plan to reach a goal	
Problem solving if your plan does not work	
Asking someone to help you reach a goal	
Surrounding yourself with people who encourage and support your goals	
Encouraging yourself to do your best	
Not quitting until your goal is reached	
Checking the progress you are making towards your goal	

Extension Activities

I Can Folder

Objective: To provide students with an opportunity to create a stamp and folder to remind them of their goal.

Materials: Blank sheet of paper, blank manila folder, old magazines, markers, scissors, and glue, p. 170, old stamps

Procedure:

- Show students some of the stamp designs that are used to commemorate accomplishments from the past. Discuss what goal each stamp represents and how reaching the goal has changed our world.

- Have students complete p. 170. Then assign them the task of designing a stamp that communicates their goal in a picture.

- When stamps are completed, provide each student with a blank manila folder and have them cut out and glue their stamp to the folder.

- Students write the following quote under their stamp:
  Consider the postage stamp. It secures success by sticking to one thing until it gets there.
  Joseph Billings

Questions to discuss: How does the quote relate to perseverance? How does your stamp communicate your goal?

Perseverance Portfolio

Objective: To provide students with an opportunity to monitor the progress they make toward becoming more persevering.

Materials: I Can Folder, student perseverance rating p. 163, student work, and p. 170

Procedure:

- Have students clip pp. 163 and 170 to the inside of their folder.

- Have students make and keep a log sheet as shown below:

Things I have done today to help me reach my goal	Things I have done today that interfered with my goal

- Allow students a few minutes at the end of each day to fill in their log sheets

- Have students keep graded work and other papers they feel show progress towards reaching their goal.

- Portfolios can be changed during the year as goals are reached and new goals are set.

Questions for Discussion: Why is it important to evaluate the progress you are making towards reaching your goal? How does your log sheet help?

Extension Activities

Adopt a Class

Objective: To provide students with an opportunity to support and encourage others to reach their goals.

Procedure:

- Discuss and brainstorm with students the different strategies and problem-solving techniques they used when they reached the goal of learning to read.

- Arrange with a first-grade teacher to adopt their class, then have your class meet with the first grade class once each week to help the younger students learn to read.

- Students can make and use flash cards of sight words, write or select books for early readers, and use other strategies that resulted from your brainstorming session.

Questions to Discuss: How does the support and encouragement of others help us persevere and reach a goal?

Perseverance in Literature

Objective: To provide students with an opportunity to read and evaluate perseverance in fiction.

Procedure:

Have students read and complete a book report on one of the following titles.

Books to choose from:

The Big Wave—Buck
Banner in the Sky—Ullman
Call it Courage—Sperry
I, Juan De Pareja—De Trevino
The Diary of a Young Girl—Frank
Shadow of a Bull—Wojciechowska
Island of the Blue Dolphins—O'Dell
Julie of the Wolves—George
Nothing is Impossible—Potter
Stone Fox—Gardiner

Hatchet—Paulsen
Weasel—DeFelice
Amelia Writes Again—Moss
Catherine Called Birdy—Cushman
Ellen Anders on Her Own—Hirsch
Bridge to Terabethia—Paterson
Dragonwings—Yep
The Cay—Taylor
Holes—Sachar
The Wheel on the School—DeJong

Notes

0-7682-2795-X *Character Education*

Notes

0-7682-2795-X *Character Education*